Large-Scale Land Acquisition in Ghana

This book examines a large-scale land acquisition project for rice production in Ghana's Volta Region, which has been purported by some to be a social and ecological showcase of a company entering a "community–private partnership" with affected communities.

Celebrated by national and international media, the project has received substantial amounts of funding from various donor organisations and claims to empower women through its much-lauded outgrower project. Although discourses of "development", "sustainability" and "women's empowerment" are used by the investment company, the state and the customary authorities to legitimise the large-scale land acquisition, this book highlights how the deal benefits mainly the powerful elite, including elite women, and generally increases the depreciation of those already most marginalised, such as poor female-headed households and settler communities that were dependent on resources from the commons now enclosed and transformed into a rice farm. The author adopts a New Institutionalist perspective in social anthropology in order to analyse how this land acquisition has been implemented in a plural institutional context and how different actors use different rules and regulations and associated legitimating discourses to increase their bargaining power and to pursue their own interests in a changing legal context. In addition, this perspective shows how benefits and losses are distributed along different intersecting axes of power, such as class, gender, clan membership and age. By focusing on power, gender and legitimisation strategies in the context of institutional change caused by the large-scale land acquisition, this book fills a gap in the literature on large-scale land acquisitions while contributing to the development of a theoretical perspective on institutional change, power relations and ideological legitimisation.

This book will be of great interest to students and scholars of land and resource grabbing, agricultural development and agribusiness, land management and development studies more broadly.

Kristina Lanz is a Senior Policy Advisor for Alliance Sud, where she works on issues relating to development cooperation, development banks and sustainable international development. Within this role, she advises federal offices, members of parliament and the federal council of Switzerland. She holds a PhD in So University of Berne, Switzerland.

T0323169

Routledge Studies in Global Land and Resource Grabbing

Series Editors: Andreas Neef and Chanrith Ngin, *The University of Auckland, New Zealand*

This series presents and discusses "resource grabbing" research in a holistic manner by addressing how the rush for land and other natural resources (water, forests, minerals, etc.) is intertwined with agriculture, mining, tourism, energy, carbon markets, climate change and disasters. This series welcomes contributions from a wide range of interdisciplinary approaches and on a global basis.

Capitalism and the Commons
Just Commons in the Era of Multiple Crises
Edited by Andreas Exner, Sarah Kumnig, and Stephan Hochleithner

Tourism, Land Grabs and Displacement
The Darker Side of the Feel-Good Industry
Andreas Neef

Agrarian Capitalism, War and Peace in Colombia
Beyond Dispossession
Jacobo Grajales

Land Grabbing and Migration in a Changing Climate
Comparative Perspectives from Senegal and Cambodia
Sara Vigil

Large-Scale Land Acquisition in Ghana
Institutional Change, Gender and Power
Kristina Lanz

For more information about this series, please visit: www.routledge.com/Routledge-Studies-in-Global-Land-and-Resource-Grabbing/book-series/GLRG

Large-Scale Land Acquisition in Ghana

Institutional Change, Gender and Power

Kristina Lanz

 Routledge
Taylor & Francis Group
LONDON AND NEW YORK

 earthscan
from Routledge

First published 2022
by Routledge
4 Park Square, Milton Park, Abingdon, Oxon OX14 4RN, UK

and by Routledge
605 Third Avenue, New York, NY 10158, USA

Routledge is an imprint of the Taylor & Francis Group, an informa business.

© 2022 Kristina Lanz

The right of Kristina Lanz to be identified as author of this work has been asserted in accordance with sections 77 and 78 of the Copyright, Designs and Patents Act 1988.

British Library Cataloguing-in-Publication Data
A catalogue record for this book is available from the British Library

Library of Congress Cataloging-in-Publication Data
A catalog record has been requested for this book

ISBN: 978-1-032-08063-5 (hbk)
ISBN: 978-1-032-08065-9 (pbk)
ISBN: 978-1-003-21276-8 (ebk)

DOI: 10.4324/9781003212768

Typeset in Times New Roman
by SPi Technologies India Pvt Ltd (Straive)

This book is dedicated to my mother, without whose support I would never have been able to embark on this journey.

Contents

Preface   viii
List of abbreviations   x

1 Introduction: land grabbing as institutional transformation   1

2 The policy context: feeding Africa while doing business –
   the anti-politics of large-scale land acquisitions   13

3 Chasing the evolutionary role of chiefs in local
   land relations   24

4 Implementation of a land deal in a plural legal setting   53

5 "They said they were bringing a development project" –
   the evolution of local livelihoods and impacts of
   the large-scale land investment   68

6 Conclusion: contested land deals, gendered power relations   108

7 Epilogue: from research to action   124

Preface

This book is based on my PhD dissertation entitled "Institutional Change, Gender and Power Relations: Case Study of a 'Best Practice' Large-scale Land Acquisition in Ghana." Research for the thesis was conducted between 2013 and 2018 and included two major research trips to Ghana in 2014 and 2016 (for 5 months and 3 months). The study design was based on a mix of qualitative methods of data collection (including participant observation, focus group discussions, semi-structured interviews with differently affected people, expert interviews and biographic interviews). Qualitative methods were favoured over quantitative methods, as in a society which revolves around oral history I felt that qualitative data would do more justice to the lived experiences of my respondents than quantitative data could. However, data was complemented by statistics and several written documents obtained from government agencies, investors and others. I also relied on the work of two MA students, who spent 3 months in the research area in 2015. In this book, I have included several maps produced by Dominic Schuppli (2016) as part of his MA thesis as well as selected quotes from interviews and group discussions conducted by Eva Schober and Dominic Schuppli. (These are marked in the book with an * and the initials of the interviewer: ES or DS.) My research would have been impossible without the help of Holy Kofi Ahiabu, my very dedicated and brilliant local research assistant, who not only translated everything that was said from Ewe to English but also brought in his own ideas and continued to stay engaged long after the research officially ended.

I am grateful to the various funding agencies that provided financial support for my PhD as well as to Prof. Tobias Haller and Prof. Jean-David Gerber, who supervised my PhD thesis, and to Prof. Elisabeth Prügl, who provided much appreciated academic support. The first two years of my PhD were funded through a Swiss Network for

International Studies (SNIS) project entitled "The effects of large-scale land acquisitions on households in rural communities of the global South: Gender relations, decision-making and food security." The third year was financed by a Swiss National Science Foundation (SNSF) project on "Large-scale land acquisitions and gender in Africa: The impact of institutional change and land investments on gender relations and food security." The final year was sponsored by a Research for Development (R4D) project, funded jointly by the SNSF and the Swiss Development Cooperation (SDC), entitled "Land commercialisation, gendered agrarian transformations and the right to food."

Abbreviations

AAGDS	Accelerated Agricultural Growth and Development Strategy
AATIF	Africa Agriculture and Trade Investment Fund
ADC	Agricultural Development Cooperation
AGRA	Alliance for a Green Revolution in Africa
AgDevCo	Agricultural Development Company
CLS	Customary Land Secretariat
CPP	Convention People's Party
CSR	Corporate Social Responsibility
DA	District Assembly
DCE	District Chief Executive
DfID	Department for International Development
DISEC	District Security Council
EIS	Environmental Impact Statement
EMP	Environmental Management Plan
ETLR	Evolutionary Theory of Land Rights
FAO	Food and Agriculture Organisation
FASDEP	Food and Agricultural Sector Development Policy
GADCO	Global Agricultural Development Company
GADS	Gender and Agricultural Development Strategy
GCAP	Ghana Commercial Agriculture Project
GHS	New Ghana Cedi
IMF	International Monetary Fund
JVA	Joint Venture Agreement
LAP	Land Administration Project
LSLA	Large-Scale Land Acquisition
LULCC	Land Use and Land Cover Change
METASIP	Medium Term Agriculture Sector Investment Plan
MoFA	Ministry of Agriculture
MP	Member of Parliament

NAFSN	New Alliance for Food Security and Nutrition
NDC	National Democratic Congress
NIE	New Institutional Economics
NPP	New Patriotic Party
PPP	Public Private Partnerships
SAP	Structural Adjustment Programme
UNDP	United Nations Development Programme
WB	World Bank

1 Introduction

Land grabbing as institutional transformation

The world is experiencing an unprecedented land rush as national elites and international investors are acquiring vast amounts of land, particularly in poorer, "land abundant" countries. As McMichael (2012, p. 690) has argued: "The conjunction of food, energy and financial crises, has resulted in international capital markets gravitating towards agriculture as a relatively safe investment haven for the relatively long-term". In an increasingly volatile climate, marked by repeated economic and financial turbulences as well as food and energy shortages, land represents a safe asset for financial speculators, multinational corporations and local businesspeople alike.

Early writing about the current land rush, generally discussed as land grabbing, was concerned with the drivers as well as with the scale of the phenomenon. Although most authors (i.e. Cotula 2012; McMichael 2012) have cited a variety of global crises as the immediate drivers, the scale of the land rush has been much contested (Borras and Franco 2013). Different authors and global and national databases arrived at highly divergent numbers of large-scale land acquisitions (LSLAs). Cotula (2013) has highlighted that some deals received much more attention than others; that is, international land investments are much more publicised than national investments, larger deals more than smaller ones. He argued that "the land rush is a fluid, fast-evolving arena where deals are signed, abandoned, redesigned or transferred at a speed that makes it difficult for inventory exercises to keep track of them" (p. 49).

Several authors (Alden Wily 2011, 2012; Peters 2013) also established the importance of analysing the recent wave of LSLAs as a long-term historical process. With reference to the African continent, Alden Wily (2011) and Cotula (2013) stated that the colonial era significantly affected the way LSLAss are negotiated today, as large tracts of land were designated as vacant by the colonial powers and vested in

DOI: 10.4324/9781003212768-1

the state, and at the same time the power of traditional chiefs was strengthened (see Chapter 3). Colonialism also set the scene for establishing Africa's role as a provider of raw materials for the global economy, a tendency that was exacerbated in the 1980s through structural adjustment programmes that further opened up African economies to foreign investment by revising land legislations and providing tax incentives and new legal protections for investors (see Chapter 2).

In policy circles, LSLAs for agricultural production continue to be promoted with the proclaimed aim of enhancing food security or energy sovereignty (Mann and Smaller 2010) or of increasing agricultural productivity and market competitiveness while reducing public spending of states (Deininger and Byerlee 2011; von Braun and Meinzen-Dick 2009). Contrary to the ambitious goals of solving rural poverty and providing smallholders with inputs and integrating them into global value chains (World Bank 2008), case study evidence of LSLAs is predominantly negative, highlighting dispossession and displacement, lack of compensation and lack of employment opportunities that characterise many agricultural investments. Several studies have shown that LSLAs create both winners and losers; although it is often local and national elites who gain most from land deals, concrete outcomes are shaped by various factors, such as class, gender, age or migration background (see, for example, Boamah and Overå 2015; Hall et al. 2015; Nyantaki-Frimpong and Bezner-Kerr 2017; Levien 2017; Lanz et al. 2018; Haller et al. 2019; Gerber and Haller 2021).

Theoretical point of departure

Whereas several scholars have stressed the increasing power of corporations, the role of (inter)national policies as well as dominant ideologies and discourses in making possible and legitimising LSLAs, others have focused on local power struggles and the consequent distribution of benefits and losses from particular land deals. The aims of the present study are to bring these strands together and to highlight how the (inter)national policy context and its related legitimating ideologies shape local power struggles and the distribution of benefits and losses at the local level. By adopting an intersectional perspective that recognises gender as one of many dimensions of power operating in any context – including (in this case study) class, migration background, social status, age and lineage – the study also seeks to add "intracategorical complexity" to the study of gender and land deals, prying open the monolithic depictions of rural "women" and "men" defined in opposition to each other (Cho et al. 2013).

For the present study, I used and adapted Ensminger's (1996) framework of institutional change, which provides a good starting point to link exogenous factors of change to "internal" dynamics of local institutional change and the distributive outcomes resulting from such changes. Ensminger's framework is based on New Institutional Economics (NIE) and has been influenced by the work of its prominent representative Douglas North. According to North (1990, p. 3): "Institutions are the rules of the game in a society or, more formally, are the humanly devised constraints that shape human interaction. In consequence, they structure incentives in human exchange, whether political, social or economic". North distinguishes between formal rules (constitutions, laws and property rights) and informal institutions (sanctions, taboos, customs, traditions and codes of conduct). NIE has been especially popular for analysing resource management and sustainability. It has been used to analyse both formal institutions for resource management (i.e. policies and property rights) (Gerber et al. 2009) and informal institutions, such as local customary rules and regulations and common property regimes (i.e. Agrawal 2003; Ensminger 1996; Haller 2010, 2013; Ostrom 1990, 2002).

Although new institutionalists often have been criticised for neglecting power relations in institutional change, Ensminger's (1996) framework addressed this concern. Her framework (see Figure 1.1) combines exogenous factors of change – such as the environment, population and technology, which all have a bearing on relative prices of different goods and services – with local institutional change and the distributional effects of this change.

In her framework of institutional change, Ensminger, like neoclassical economists, emphasises that changing relative prices lead to institutional change. However, this change is filtered through the local political system (constituted of ideology, bargaining power, institutions

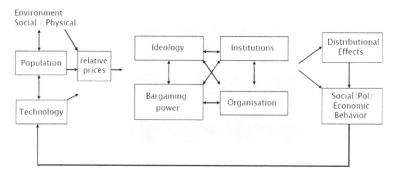

Figure 1.1 Framework of institutional change.

Source: Ensminger 1996, p. 10

and organisations) and consequently its outcomes are much less certain than neoclassical economists would predict (i.e. they do not necessarily lead to the most efficient outcomes). In accordance with this, Ensminger beholds that although "such change may be in the direction of increasing the economic benefit of the powerful parties who initiate the change, there is no reason to expect that these interests will be consistent with increasing economic output for society as a whole" (p. 166).

Her case study of the Orma society in Kenya shows that the way in which institutions are re-created and changed usually represents the interests of those with the most bargaining power, which derives from social status, wealth and the ability to manipulate ideology. As a consequence, "institutional change usually creates both winners and losers", and "winners have an obvious interest in promoting such change; losers have an interest in resisting it" (ibid., p. 166). The model was extended by Haller (2010, 2013), who elaborated the concept of ideology to include discourses and narratives, which are used by different actors to increase their bargaining power and to justify the selection, transformation or crafting of new institutions.

Ensminger (1996, pp. 10–11) highlights how economists generally focus on those aspects outside the black box and their impacts on relative prices, treating factors inside the black box as endogenous and unchanging. She argues that, in contrast, anthropologists have tended to neglect the role of relative prices and rather focused on aspects inside the black box to explain economic behaviour and distributional effects. She suggests merging the two and "shift[ing] back and forth, sometimes trying to understand the effect of demography and environment on relative prices, sometimes focusing on the effect of relative prices on ideology and institutions or the effect of ideology on institutions and vice versa" (p. 10). My case study confirms that especially in a context of increasing global interest in land, which manifests itself locally in LSLAs, rising prices of land can be seen as a key trigger for institutional change.

Even though the external variables listed in Ensminger's model (environment, population and technology) are certainly important parameters for changing relative prices of land (or other goods and services), the aim of this book is to draw attention to the importance of another external variable: the national policy context. A favourable (inter)national institutional context and the use of ideological legitimation are what make LSLAs possible and thus contribute to rising relative prices of land locally. Through rising investor interest in land which leads to rising relative prices of land and thus to increased LSLAs, this policy context and its related legitimating ideologies, discourses and narratives become relevant locally.

Because the LSLA itself represents a shift from common to private property, I will briefly outline the different types of property and explain the consequences that such a shift entails. I will then discuss the role of power and ideology in institutional change. Building on Haller's (2010, 2013) adaptation of Ensminger's model of institutional change, I will differentiate ideology from discourses and narratives and discuss how these are used to legitimate certain institutions. Drawing on Feminist and Gender Studies, I will highlight that gender is a crucial variable of institutional change. Finally, I will introduce my adapted model of institutional change, which takes into account the (inter)national policy context.

Different types of property and the shift from common to private property

The literature on property rights usually distinguishes between four types of property regimes: open-access, common property, state or public property and private property. Whereas open-access is in essence a "no property" regime, as there are no clearly defined rights and regulations, all other property regimes need to be backed by an authority, who defends the rights of property owners in order to be effective (Bromley 1992, p. 12). Property needs to be titled, registered, protected and enforced in order to make accumulation, as the basis of capitalism, possible. Thus, it is not surprising that common property regimes all over the world have come under threat as capitalism has expanded globally.

Common property regimes often are confounded with open-access regimes, where no rules or regulations exist to protect resources from over-exploitation. As a consequence, it is argued that land not managed by the state or held privately is bound to be over-exploited by rational individuals seeking to maximise their own gain, thus leading to a "tragedy of the commons" (Hardin 1968). However, various authors have highlighted that these types of open-access situations are very rare and that most so-called "open-access" resources belong to specified local groups (villages, lineages or kinship groups) and that there are indeed rules and regulations governing the use of these resources (Acheson 1989; McCabe 1990).

Under common property, the same plot of land often is used for different purposes by different user groups, giving rise to the notion of these groups possessing different bundles of rights (Meinzen-Dick and Mwangi 2008). A common typology of rights has been suggested by Schlager and Ostrom (1992), who distinguish the following: access, withdrawal, management, exclusion and alienation. Individual families frequently move their plots and retract and expand them according to various factors, such as soil fertility, labour availability, number of farmers, and resource conflicts (Haller 2013). Who has which rights and which decision-making power in a given common property system is based on gender, ethnicity, religion or wealth and thus also on power relations (Agrawal 2003, p. 251).

Although Elinor Ostrom's seminal work has shown how these locally devised rules and regulations are in many cases more appropriate and effective at protecting resources from overuse than state or private property rules (Ostrom 1990), the "tragedy of the commons" is still evoked by advocates of privatisation. Private property is also seen as a means of cutting transaction costs, as the use of the land is decided by the owner without the need for complex negotiations amongst different resource users (Acheson 1989). This approach is backed by the very influential work of economist Hernando De Soto (2000), who argues that poverty stems not from a lack of resources but rather from the absence of property rights. According to him, the poor hold a lot of "dead capital" – land and other resources, which owing to the lack of legally sanctioned property rights, they cannot collateralise in order to get credit. Land titling thus is commonly promoted as the solution to over-exploitation of resources and at the same time is heralded as the best way to allocate land to the most efficient users, thus creating economic growth (see Chapter 2). Land titling is also a primary means to encourage large-scale land investments.

However, even in contexts where there are no private property titles – as in the case of many African countries, including Ghana – LSLAs have been highly prevalent, often encouraged by governments claiming that lands held under common property are "wastelands" waiting to be developed (see Alden Wily 2012). In these cases, LSLAs by foreign investors imply a de facto privatisation of land that was previously held under common property. In order to understand how institutional change from common to private property occurs, it is important to exemplify the role of power and ideology (see Ensminger 1996; Haller 2010, 2013).

The role of power and ideology in institutional change

Ensminger (1996, p. 7) defines bargaining power as "one's ability to get what one wants from others. It may come from greater wealth or social position or the ability to manipulate the ideology of others". Although wealth and social position are important determinants of power, Ribot and Peluso (2003) have identified a number of relational and structural sources of power ("bundles of power"), which may also have a bearing on people's ability to influence institutional change. These include access to technology, capital, markets, labour, knowledge and authority as well as individual markers of identity (such as gender, age or status) and social relations.

As mentioned in Ensminger's definition, power is also inextricably linked to ideology. According to Ensminger (1996, p. 2), ideology "refers to the values and beliefs that determine people's goals and shape their choices". Haller (2010, 2013) and Galvin and Haller (2008) elaborate on Ensminger's model by differentiating ideologies from discourses and narratives, which are used by different actors explaining and legitimating institutional choices and changes. They define ideologies as worldviews that give orientation to people's actions and perceptions, discourses as the production of meaning and orientation through spoken and written language, and narratives as the logical definition and explanation of specific situations (Galvin and Haller 2008, p. 14).

The role of ideologies in creating legitimacy has been delineated by Tyler (2005, p. 211) as "legitimating ideologies" (which he also calls "legitimating myths") – a term that I also adopt in this book. Legitimating ideologies are defined as a set of "normative justifications for existing policies and practices through which they are seen as appropriate, reasonable and fair and are, consequently, more readily accepted" (p. 211). Tyler (2005, p. 215) argues that

> when there is a widely accepted set of legitimating myths that validate some social arrangement or set of social practices, it is difficult for a group that is disadvantaged to create the conditions by which it can bring itself together and develop an alternative ideology that it can then put forward to society.

The main legitimating ideology of importance in the context of LSLAs is the ideology of modernisation and development, which evolved in the U.S. during the Cold War era as a response to the perceived communist threat. According to modernisation theory, a linear process from "under-developed" and "traditional" societies towards "developed" societies based on Western values and institutions is presumed (see Latham 2000). Gordon (1989, p. 183) highlights that "modernization and development theories were more politically sensitive modifications of the colonial ideology, which characterized colonized societies as backward and inferior to the dynamic, industrial West". He goes on to argue that the "promotion of capital-intensive industry, foreign investment, Western 'aid', and heavy borrowing would also render the poor countries more pliable by making them dependent on Western technology, goods, expertise, and finance" (ibid., pp. 183–184). This is in line with Ferguson's (1994) "anti-politics machine" of development. He argues that, based on the dominant ideology of progress through modernisation, non-governmental organisations and other development actors have constructed discourses and narratives, which see poverty and under-development as technical problems to be solved through their interventions, thus leading to a de-politicisation of "development".

However, legitimating ideologies, discourses and narratives not only are used by powerful states or corporations to legitimate their interventions but also – in line with Ensminger's framework – are evoked strategically by local actors striving to further their own interests in institutional change. The use of specific discourses in a local context has also been analysed by Hagmann and Péclard (2010) in their work on state-building processes in Africa. They argue that, parallel to material resources, different actors mobilise symbolic repertoires to further their interests, legitimise their actions and mobilise popular support. These repertoires are embedded in strong discourses as sources of legitimacy and may build on international discourses, such as "democracy", "development", "sustainability" or "human rights", as well as on notions of national, religious or cultural identity (Hagmann and Péclard 2010, p. 547). In their case study of institutional change in Zambia, Haller and Merten (2008) highlight how powerful individuals refer to both customary rules and regulations (based on the ideology of "tradition") or statutory rules and regulations (based on the ideology of modernity and discourses of citizenship, democracy and development) to legitimate certain institutional arrangements. The authors describe this as a strategy of "institution shopping".

Gendered institutional change

Gender, as a socially constructed identity, alongside and in conjunction with other variables such as race, class, age or migration background, is a key characteristic of power relations across scales. Although Gender Studies have inadvertently contributed to create a simplified narrative of men as perpetrators and women as victims – whereby women's bargaining power both in society at large and in the household is always subordinated to men's – this view has been challenged by postcolonial feminist researchers (i.e. Mohanty 1984; Narayan 1997), who have criticised Western feminists' representations of women in "Third World" countries as stereotyped and homogenous and have emphasised the need to be conscious of the politics of specific locations and of differences between women with regard to class, age, sexuality, migration background and so on. Intersectionality Studies, in turn, have gone one step further by focusing on "the institutional power arrangements that make [specific] identities invisible and illegible" (Cooper 2016, p. 9). Different authors have analysed the way that multiple categories of social identity, such as age, nation, religion, ability, sexuality and migration background, interact to create specific forms of social marginalisation in specific places. Recognising multiple axes of identity serves to make visible the negative impacts of specific institutions on particular people's bargaining power.

While adopting an intersectional perspective to analyse the outcomes of a specific LSLA in Ghana, this book will also highlight how references to gender equality and women's empowerment are becoming more and more embedded in neoliberal market ideology and increasingly are used to legitimise diverse policy interventions aimed at facilitating LSLAs. This "neoliberalisation of feminism" has also been pointed out by several feminist scholars (Cornwall et al. 2007; Prügl 2015, 2016; Roberts 2015; Lanz et al. 2019), who – while focusing on different policy areas – are all concerned with an obvious "dynamic of appropriation and incorporation that constantly subverts and depletes transformational feminist agendas" (Mama 2004, p. 121).

An adapted framework of institutional change

By adapting Ensminger's framework (1996), I focus on the national policy context (which is embedded in and shaped by its historically specific international policy context) as an exogenous factor which influences relative prices and makes LSLA possible (see Figure 1.2). Following the framework, I argue that the LSLA acts as a vector through which this (inter)national policy context and its related legitimating ideologies, discourses and narratives are activated and become relevant locally. Although – as outlined in Figure 1.2 – the development of national (as well as international) policies could also be analysed as a struggle between various actors and organisations with different bargaining power, using diverse institutions and ideologies to promote certain policies, this is beyond the scope of the present book. My main focus is thus on the relationship between specific institutions and the ideologies, discourses and narratives used to legitimise these institutional arrangements. I aim to show how, through LSLA, they become relevant and are used by diverse actors in the local context, thus shaping the distribution of benefits and losses of the LSLA.

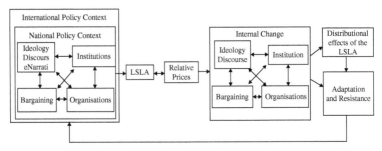

Figure 1.2 Adapted framework of institutional change. (Adapted from Ensminger 1996)

References

Acheson, J. (1989). 'Management of common-property resources'. In Platteau, J. (ed.), *Economic anthropology*. Stanford, CA: Stanford University Press, pp. 351–78.

Agrawal, A. (2003). 'Sustainable governance of common-pool resources: Context, methods, and politics'. *Annual Review of Anthropology* 32: 243–62.

Alden Wily, L. (2011). 'The law is to blame. The vulnerable status of common property rights in sub-Saharan Africa'. *Development and Change* 42 (3): 357–79.

Alden Wily, L. (2012). 'Looking back to see forward: The legal niceties of land theft in land rushes'. *Journal of Peasant Studies* 39 (3–4): 751–75.

Boamah, F. and R. Overå (2015). 'Rethinking livelihood impacts of biofuel land deals in Ghana'. *Development and Change* 47 (1): 98–129.

Borras Jr., S.M. and J. Franco (2013). 'Global land grabbing and political reactions "from below"'. *Third World Quarterly* 34 (9): 1723–47.

Bromley, D. (1992). 'The commons, common property and environmental policy'. *Environmental and Resource Economics* (2): 1–17.

Cho, S., Crenshaw, K.W., and L. McCall. (2013). 'Toward a field of intersectionality studies: Theory, applications, and praxis'. *Signs: Journal of Women in Culture and Society* 38 (4): 785–810.

Cooper, B. (2016). 'Intersectionality'. In Disch, L. and M. Mawkesworth (eds.), *The Oxford Handbook of Feminist Theory*. Oxford, UK: Oxford University Press.

Cornwall, A., Harrison, E. and A. Whitehead (2007). 'Gender myths and feminist fables'. *Development and Change* 38: 1–20.

Cotula, L. (2012). 'The international political economy of the global land rush: A critical appraisal of trends, scale, geography and drivers'. *Journal of Peasant Studies* 39 (3–4): 649–80.

Cotula, L. (2013). *The great African land grab? Agricultural investments and the global food system*. London: Zed Books.

Deininger, K. and D. Byerlee (2011). *Rising global interest in farmland: Can it yield sustainable and equitable benefits?* Washington, DC: World Bank.

De Soto, H. (2000). *The mystery of capital: Why capitalism triumphs in the West and fails everywhere else.* New York: Basic Books.

Ensminger, J. (1996). *Making a market: The institutional transformation of an African society.* Cambridge, UK: Cambridge University Press.

Ferguson, J. (1994). *The anti-politics machine: "Development", depoliticization and bureaucratic power in Lesotho.* Minneapolis: University of Minnesota Press.

Galvin, M. and T. Haller (2008). *People, protected areas and global change: Participatory conservation in Latin America, Africa, Asia and Europe.* NCCR North-South. Berne, Switzerland: Geographica Bernensia.

Gerber, J.D. and T. Haller (2021). 'The drama of the grabbed commons: Anti-politics machine and local responses'. *Journal of Peasant Studies* 48 (6): 1304–27. doi:10.1080/03066150.2020.1758673

Gerber, J.D., Knoepfel, P., Nahrath, S. and F. Varone (2009). 'Institutional resource regimes: Towards sustainability through the combination of property-rights theory and policy analysis'. *Ecological Economics* 68 (3): 798–809.

Gordon, A. (1989). 'The myth of modernization and development'. *Sociological Spectrum* 9 (2): 175–95.

Hagmann, T. and D. Péclard (2010). 'Negotiating statehood: Dynamics of power and domination in Africa'. *Development and Change* 41 (4): 539–62.

Hall, R., Scoones, I. and D. Tsikata (eds.) (2015). *Africa's land rush: Rural livelihoods and agrarian change.* Woolbridge, UK: James Currey.

Haller, T., ed. (2010). *Disputing the floodplains: Institutional change and the politics of resource management in African floodplains.* Leiden, The Netherlands: Brill.

Haller, T. (2013). *The contested floodplain: Institutional change of the commons in the Kafue Flats, Zambia.* Lanham, MD: Rowman & Littlefield.

Haller, T. and S. Merten (2008). '"We are Zambians – Don't tell us how to fish!" Institutional change, power relations and conflicts in the Kafue Flats fisheries in Zambia'. *Human Ecology* 36 (5): 699–715.

Haller, T. et al. (2019). 'Large scale land acquisition as commons grabbing: A comparative study on cases from Africa'. In Lozny, L. and T. McGivern (eds.), *Global perspectives on long term community resource management.* Berlin, New York: Springer, pp. 125–64.

Hardin, G. (1968). 'The tragedy of the commons'. *Science* 162: 1243–48.

Lanz, K., Gerber, J.D. and T. Haller (2018). 'Large-scale land acquisitions and agricultural intensification in Ghana: Customary authorities at the meeting point of tradition and modernization'. *Development and Change* 49 (6): 1526–52.

Lanz, K., Prügl, E. and J.D. Gerber (2019). 'Gender, chiefs, and power: Case study of a large-scale land investment in Ghana'. *Journal of Peasant Studies* 47 (3): 535–43.

Latham, M.E. (2000). *Modernization as ideology: American social science and 'nation- building' in the Kennedy era.* Chapel Hill, NC: University of North Carolina Press.

Levien, M. (2017). 'Gender and land dispossession'. *Journal of Peasant Studies* 44 (6): 1111–34.

Mama, A. (2004). 'Demythologising gender in development: Feminist studies in African contexts'. *IDS Bulletin* 35 (4): 121–24.

Mann, H. and C. Smaller (2010). *Foreign land purchases for agriculture: What impact on sustainable development?* Sustainable Development Innovation Brief. New York: United Nations.

McCabe, T.J. (1990). 'Turkana pastoralism: A case against the tragedy of the commons'. *Human Ecology* 18 (1): 81–103.

McMichael, P. (2012). 'The land grab and corporate food regime restructuring'. *Journal of Peasant Studies* 39 (3–4): 681–701.

Meinzen-Dick, R. and E. Mwangi (2008). 'Cutting the web of interests'. *Land Use Policy* 26: 36–43.

Mohanty, C. (1984). 'Under Western eyes: Feminist scholarship and colonial discourses'. *Boundary* 2: 333–58.

Narayan, U. (1997). *Dislocating cultures: Identities, traditions, and third world feminism*. New York: Routledge.

North, D. (1990). *Institutions, institutional change and economic performance*. Cambridge, UK: Cambridge University Press.

Nyantaki-Frimpong, H. and R. Bezner-Kerr (2017). 'Land grabbing, social differentiation, intensified migration and food security in Northern Ghana'. *Journal of Peasant Studies* 44 (2): 421–44.

Ostrom, E. (1990). *Governing the commons: The evolution of institutions for collective action*. Cambridge, UK: Cambridge University Press.

Ostrom, E., ed. (2002). *The drama of the commons*. Washington, DC: National Academy Press.

Peters, P. (2013). 'Conflicts over land and threats to customary tenure in Africa'. *African Affairs* 112 (449): 543–62.

Prügl, E. (2015). 'Neoliberalising feminism'. *New Political Economy* 20 (4): 614–31.

Prügl, E. (2016). 'Neoliberalism with a feminist face: Crafting a new hegemony at the World Bank'. *Feminist Economics* 23 (1): 30–53.

Ribot, J.C. and N.L. Peluso (2003). 'A theory of access'. *Rural Sociology* 68 (2): 153–81.

Roberts, A. (2015). 'The political economy of "transnational business feminism": Problematizing the corporate-led gender equality agenda'. *International Feminist Journal of Politics* 17 (2): 209–31.

Schlager, E. and E. Ostrom (1992). 'Property-rights regimes and natural resources: A conceptual analysis'. *Land Economics* 68 (3): 249–62.

Tyler, T.R. (2005). 'Introduction: Legitimating ideologies'. *Social Justice Research* 18: 211–15.

von Braun, J. and R. Meinzen-Dick (2009). *"Land Grabbing" by foreign investors in developing countries: Risks and opportunities*. Washington, DC: IFPRI.

World Bank (2008). *The world development report 2008: Agriculture for development*. Washington, DC: World Bank.

2 The policy context
Feeding Africa while doing business – the anti-politics of large-scale land acquisitions

Structural adjustment and beyond: roll-back of the state and increased corporate control

As African nations declared independence in the 1960s and 1970s, an era of state-led development followed. At the height of the Cold War, the international community financed autocratic regimes with vast state bureaucracies, leading to a huge indebtedness of numerous newly independent nations (Hoogvelt 1997). In exchange for new loans, most African countries in the 1980s agreed to adopt a number of structural adjustment programmes (SAPs) promoted by the International Monetary Fund (IMF) and the World Bank. These measures focused on privatisation, liberalisation and export commodity production and sought to promote "open and free competitive market economies, supervised by minimal states" (Hoogvelt 1997, p. 181). Various authors have pointed out how, as a result, African states have become increasingly "weak" or "hollowed out" (Ferguson 2006; Hoogvelt 1997). This roll-back of the state also led to a proliferation of non-governmental organisations (NGOs) and other development actors who took over many of the state's functions, simultaneously leading to a de-politicisation of development (Ferguson 2006). Towards the end of the 1980s, as the failures of structural adjustment were becoming clear political conditionalities (under the term "good governance") were added to the donor agenda, resulting in widespread propaganda of democratisation and decentralisation across Africa. At the same time, many of the substantial economic policies advocated by international donors were "insulated from processes of representative democracy" (Ferguson 2006, p. 13).

In the 1980s and 1990s, development aid to African countries – much of which was directed at policy reforms – grew exponentially, while African countries themselves (it has been argued) mostly stagnated or

DOI: 10.4324/9781003212768-2

even became poorer in the same time span. This has often been attributed to weak state structures and corruption (Reno 2000; Rotberg 2004).
Van de Walle (2001) convincingly describes the effects of neo-patrimonial tendencies in African states, which are characterised (despite decentralisation efforts) by centralised state control, the abuse of state resources for private gain and clientelistic tendencies. Lund (2006, p. 685) also emphasises that the capacity of decentralised statutory institutions "to define and enforce collectively binding decisions on members of society" is generally weak. Even though state bureaucracies often are understaffed and operating on few resources, several authors highlight the active role of states since connections to the governing ruling elite are of crucial importance not only to local elites wishing to gain access to contracts and resources but also to foreign investors, NGOs and donor agencies, which rely on the state to do business (Reno 1998). As Kassimir (2001, p. 111) points out, "the state is rarely irrelevant in the way transboundary connections are formed and institutionalized". Ferguson (2006, p. 207) goes even further by arguing that the core feature of African states' sovereignty today is not effective control over their territories or the monopoly on the use of violence but rather "to provide contractual legal authority that can legitimate the extractive work of transnational firms".

Agriculture and food production were also transformed under structural adjustment. While SAPs "systematically attacked all aspects of state-centered development" and "paved the way for both global markets in edible commodities and transnational supply chains" (Friedmann 2005, p. 256), "a massive wave of mergers and consolidations swept the U.S. and the world" (ibid., p. 250). Since then, transnational agro-industrial corporations backed by powerful agrochemical conglomerates providing specialised inputs, such as bio-engineered seeds, fertilizers and pesticides, have increasingly conquered new territories and spheres of influence. The introduction of agrochemicals has completely transformed the nature of agricultural production in many African societies, and SAPs often had disastrous effects, especially in the area of food security, as the export focus of agricultural production led to food shortages and hunger in numerous countries, the consequences of which were mostly borne disproportionately by women (Hoogvelt 1997).

"Public–private partnerships" for commercial agriculture and the legitimation of large-scale land acquisitions

In the promotion of commercial agriculture, the last decade has seen a renewed engagement of international donors, who are now influencing

African state policy through a number of "public–private partner-ships" (PPPs) – commitments between African governments, donor agencies and private corporations – such as the New Alliance for Food Security and Nutrition (NAFSN), the Alliance for a Green Revolution in Africa (AGRA) and the Millennium Challenge Corporation (MCC) (Borras et al. 2013). Effectively facilitating large-scale land acquisi-tions for agricultural purposes through different policy propositions (such as land reforms and seed laws), these initiatives usually justify their interventions by arguing that land acquisitions can bring much-needed development to local communities in terms of infrastructure, job creation and increased food production (Deininger 2011; von Braun and Meinzen-Dick 2009). More recent policy initiatives spe-cifically focus on integrating smallholders into value chains, such as through outgrower schemes, which are commonly portrayed as "win–win" scenarios (McMichael 2012).

Through the NAFSN – which brings together a wide range of mul-tinational corporations (such as Yara, Monsanto and Nestlé), devel-opment agencies from G8 countries, the World Bank, the Gates Foundation and 10 African governments (including Ghana's) – par-taking governments have committed to investment-friendly policy reforms in exchange for funding pledges from the participating corpo-rations and development agencies. AGRA, MCC and other PPPs also focus on market-based solutions to food security by promoting land privatisation and outgrower schemes or by providing agrochemical inputs and certified seeds to farmers (McMichael 2012, p. 695). McMichael goes as far as stating that "[s]uch development 'services' constitute a broad infrastructural complex supporting land grabbing – both material and ideological" (ibid., p. 696), whereby the ideological component consists in disguising corporate control and profit by declaring it as development, poverty reduction and food security.

Just add women and stir

As the focus of development has shifted from state actors to private actors and the nature of neoliberalism has changed from state-organ-ised to transnationally organised, feminist ideas have also gained traction in a variety of fora (Fraser 2009). An analysis of funding for women's rights by the Association of Women in Development shows that "women and girls" have become a (rhetorical) priority in nearly every funding sector – parallel to the upsurge of private sector actors in development and the corporatisation of development agendas and financing (Arutyunova and Clark 2013).

As such, gender rhetoric has also entered the neoliberal agenda of agricultural commercialisation, where women are considered to hold "the key to food security" and to play a major role in "ensuring food security in the developing world" (Quisumbing et al. 1995). Scholarly findings that women are more likely to use their incomes to invest in family nutrition (i.e. Doss 2006) provide a key legitimating narrative for these women-centered projects, as they promise to increase household food security by giving women access to monetary resources and connecting them to the market. Gender thus also appears prominently in the proclaimed objectives of the NAFSN, which in 2013 endorsed an accountability and monitoring framework that consisted of three outcomes: "(1) improved enabling environment for investment, (2) increased responsible private sector investment in agriculture, and (3) increased agriculture sector growth"[1]. The three objectives were related to three aggregate impacts: "poverty reduction, improved food and nutrition security and economic empowerment of women" (McKeon 2014, p. 13).

This new rationale of inserting women into processes of agrarian commercialisation follows a logic that feminists have called "add women and stir". Claims to empowerment are reduced to counting how many women have been included in commercial ventures but without questioning the quality of jobs. But, as Fraser (2009) argues, the integration of countless women into labour markets across the globe constitutes "a new romance of female advancement and gender justice" while turning a blind eye to the often precarious and highly flexible working conditions as well as the double burden of reproductive and productive work (Fraser 2009, p. 110). Steeped in neoliberal logics equating development with modernisation through economic growth, this integration aims to "make markets work for women" while claiming to empower women so that they can work in markets (Prügl 2016).

Land reform as a prerequisite for foreign investment

Clearly demarcated land rights are demanded by investors in order to guarantee security for their investments. So it is not surprising that a wave of land-titling initiatives swept the African continent in the 1980s and 1990s. Land titling was and continues to be promoted as a way of creating land tenure security which is supposed to encourage investment and lead to the creation of a free land market. This is supposed to lead to the allocation of land to the most efficient users, thus creating economic growth (de Soto 2000). Thus, the World Bank's prescription in the 1980s and early 1990s was to "replace customary systems with titling and private property rights, which were posited as the necessary pre-conditions for modernization and development" (Peters 2009, p. 1318). As has been shown in a broad literature review by Peters (2009), these land reforms often had disastrous effects, as they "frequently exacerbated conflicts by ignoring overlapping and multiple rights and uses of land, and led to reinforced patterns of unequal access to land based on gender, age, ethnicity and class" (p. 1318).

Since most land-titling initiatives failed, in the 1990s prominent development organisations, such as the World Bank, started to change their thinking (or at least their rhetoric) based on an "Evolutionary Theory of Land Rights" (ETLR), whereby it was assumed that "indigenous land rights, under the impulse of market forces, are capable of significant autonomous evolution in a beneficial (efficiency-enhancing) direction", which eventually will culminate in a private property system (Platteau 1996, p. 30). However, according to the ETLR, governments must play a central role in this evolutionary process, as these changes "need to be supported by a governmental intervention designed to formalize and consolidate the newly emerging system of private property rights" (ibid., p. 30). This idea, which is legitimised as a "pro-poor land reform", forms the basis of numerous current donor interventions in African countries and is designed to strengthen and formalise customary land rights on both a collective and an individual basis.

Alongside this shift to customary land tenure, increasing attention has been drawn to women's land rights (Razavi 2003). Ravnborg et al. (2016, p. 416) show that, whereas previous land reforms generally were characterised by gender-blind language (assuming that if land were titled in the name of the head-of-household, the whole household would benefit), recent policy documents specifically emphasise the significance of women's land rights. Aid agencies have published a number of documents to point out the importance of integrating women's land rights into current land tenure reforms[2]. Some of these documents emphasise the moral values of having greater gender equality, and others are based on purely utilitarian arguments which tie women's empowerment to increased development efficiency and economic growth (Ravnborg et al. 2016).

Even though recent land reforms generally contain provisions against the discrimination of women and "gender equity is a key theme in the presentation of the reforms" (Federici 2011, p. 45), the turn to customary land rights has been challenged by feminist organisations and researchers across Africa who argue that it is incompatible with greater gender equality (Whitehead and Tsikata 2003). These critics showcase the patriarchal nature of most customary systems, where women generally have only "secondary rights" to land; that is, they generally receive access to land through their relationship to their father or husband and in many instances also lose access to their husband's land in case of death or divorce (Whitehead and Tsikata 2003). Although, under customary tenure and conditions of land abundance, women may have guaranteed access to land through their kinship group, their land rights tend to become vulnerable when land becomes scarce or valuable (Berry 1993).

Ghana's agricultural policy in historical context

Even though Ghana was one of the first countries to declare independence (1957), its economy still depended a great deal on exports to Great Britain (Duncan 2004). Under Kwame Nkrumah, the development of state-led, large-scale industrial agriculture thus became a policy objective. However, owing to heavy resistance by chiefs, the policy objective of replacing small-scale agriculture with large-scale industrial agriculture was not achieved (see Chapter 3).

In 1966, the Nkrumah government was overthrown by a military coup – the first of four military coups and nine changes in government between 1966 and 1981. During the Acheampong military regime in the 1970s, a new approach to agriculture was developed with guidance and aid from the World Bank. It focused on the formation of large-scale industrial agriculture – especially the cultivation of oil palm, cocoa, cotton and tobacco as well as rice and vegetables – and included the establishment of large plantations and the involvement of outgrowers. The Special Scheme for Participation in Agriculture aimed to encourage foreign and transnational capital to invest in agriculture. The state helped with land acquisitions and the provision of infrastructure, but investments had to have at least 40% Ghanaian ownership and investors were obliged to create outgrower schemes. According to Amanor (1999, p. 37),

> outgrower schemes were written into these projects as a means of camouflaging the expropriation of land, by appearing to give farmers a role in new development projects, but also as a means of creating levers by introducing contract farming and integrating peasant farms as a source of low-cost labour for agribusiness.

Although only 12 companies participated in this special scheme and most of them dropped out after a few years, the expropriation of land was significant. The compulsory acquisition of land by the state – necessary for the establishment of these ventures – was again met with heavy resistance by traditional authorities in several locations (Tsikata and Yaro 2014).

The changes that had been introduced in the 1970s were cemented and expanded in the 1980s under structural adjustment. In 1981, Flight Lieutenant Jerry Rawlings took power in a military coup. He implemented one of Africa's first and most far-reaching SAPs. Adjustment policies promoted by the World Bank and the IMF included the removal of subsidies for inputs and seeds, the removal of protective tariffs on imported food, and the divestment of state enterprises and the promotion of foreign investment in agriculture through extensive tax concessions and other policy measures (Amanor 1999). As a result of the conducive policy environment, various investments, especially in exotic fruit crops such as bananas, mangoes and pineapples, were made. But the promotion of export crops, the increased competition from cheap food imports, and the rising costs of seeds and other farm inputs served to undermine local food production, leading to widespread hunger and malnutrition (Cornia et al. 1987). It has been argued that women, who made up a large part of food producers and traders, were particularly hurt by these changes (Duncan 2004).

Current agricultural policy: encouraging large-scale commercial agriculture remains key

Although structural adjustment in Ghana opened up the economy to foreign investment and paved the way for the increasing commoditisation of natural resources and the environment, the general agricultural policy orientation has remained the same. Even though Ghanaian policies usually are elaborated through a consultative process, including different stakeholders, the policy elaboration process often is led and financed by donor agencies and the general policy directions are in line with international commitments, such as Ghana's commitment to the NAFSN. Various policy documents thus emphasise the government's strategy of opening up the country to foreign investment in agriculture and the promotion of export crops over food crops (i.e. Ghana Vision 2020 and the Accelerated Agricultural Growth and Development Strategy (AAGDS)). The AAGDS, passed in 2001, emphasised for the first time the need to strive for gender equity in agriculture and to promote women's access to land and agricultural resources.

The current Food and Agricultural Sector Development Policy (FASDEP) and its related Medium-Term Agriculture Sector Investment Plan (METASIP) are endorsed and supported by the NAFSN with a pledge of over USD $584 million to help the Ghanaian government fulfil its policy commitments. Key commitments made by the government include commercialising the seed sector, creating a secure investment climate for investors – for example, by establishing a database on suitable land – and implementing "pilot model lease agreements" (i.e. through outgrower schemes) (see Department for International Development [DfID] 2013).

FASDEP also places great emphasis on gender equality and commits the relevant agencies to mainstream gender in all programmes and policies according to the Gender and Agricultural Development Strategy (GADS). Policy elaboration was funded by the World Bank and various other donors (i.e. FAO, Canadian Aid, GIZ, Oxfam etc.) were also engaged. In order to take account of the new policy environment, new objectives, including the promotion of gender-responsive agri-business, value addition and market access for growth in incomes, were introduced. The general focus of GADS is on providing women with access to various resources (including income, employment and markets) as well as ensuring that decision-making bodies and agricultural projects are made up of at least 40% women.

The implementation of these agricultural policies is in the hands of the Ministry of Agriculture and the District Directorates of Agriculture with their agricultural extension officers. Districts commit themselves to develop their District Development Plans according to the objectives of FASDEP while taking the specific situation of the District into account. Plans have to be developed in consultation with the private sector and NGOs, and policies often are elaborated and implemented through donor-funded projects, such as the Ghana Commercial Agriculture Project (GCAP), one of Ghana's flagship projects in the promotion of commercial agriculture. GCAP is a USD $145 million Government of Ghana project funded jointly by the World Bank and the United States Agency for International Development (USAID) and aims to develop the commercial agriculture sector in Ghana. It initially focused on establishing PPPs and providing matching grants to private companies aimed at supporting Ghana's "commercial agriculture renaissance": developing large irrigation canals, facilitating land acquisition, supporting and extending nucleus farms for the benefits of smallholders and outgrowers, expanding infrastructure into outgrower lands, and promoting a secure investment climate that focuses on access to land (GCAP website, last accessed: 21 February 2018).

The PPP focus was dropped because not enough companies were interested in partnering with the government, but at the time of research in 2016, 31 nucleus outgrower projects, including the Global Agri-Development Company (GADCO), had benefitted from GCAP matching grants (see Chapter 4). The key requirements for companies to access GCAP funding were that they had to provide at least 20% of the needed funds themselves, work with outgrowers and be engaged in the cultivation of one of the GCAP priority crops (i.e. rice, maize, soya or horticultural crops). Furthermore, all projects were supposed to comply with World Bank environmental and social safeguard requirements, which include undergoing a comprehensive Environmental and Social Impact Assessment and having an Environmental Management Plan.

In 2015, the GCAP also developed a series of three documents to guide investors and communities when acquiring large tracts of land for commercial agriculture. GCAP also took gender considerations into account since World Bank requirements foresaw that all projects should support women and other vulnerable groups. For GCAP, this meant that female outgrowers had to make up at least 40% of all outgrower operations and that nucleus farms should also employ women. However, according to the GCAP representative and the WIAD (Women in Aid & Development) representative, who was in charge of monitoring, not all farms complied with these criteria.

Although Ghana's agricultural policy thus is increasingly shaped and influenced by international actors, the way that these policies are implemented and translated in a local context is heavily shaped by local institutions and power relations, as will be highlighted in the following chapters.

Notes

1 For example, as of 3 October 2017, the New Alliance for Food Security and Nutrition reported on its website on the progress that has been made as a result of the partnership and highlights that "private investments have reached 8.2 million smallholders and created more than 21,000 jobs in 2014, over half of which were for women".
2 See, for example, the *World Bank Gender in Agriculture Sourcebook* (2009) and the *Toolkit for Integrating Gender-Related Issues in Land Policy and Administration Projects* (World Bank 2013).

References

Amanor, K.S. (1999). *Global restructuring and land rights in Ghana: Forest food chains, timber and rural livelihoods*. Uppsala, Sweden: Nordiska Africa Institute.
Arutyunova, A. and C. Clark (2013). *Watering the leaves, starving the roots*. Toronto, ON: AWID.
Berry, S. (1993). *No condition is permanent: The social dynamics of agrarian change in sub- Saharan Africa*. Madison, WI: The University of Wisconsin Press.
Borras Jr., S.M., Franco, J.C. and C. Wang (2013). 'The challenge of global governance of land grabbing: Changing international agricultural context and competing political views and strategies'. *Globalizations* 10 (1): 161–79.

Cornia, G.A., Jolly, R. and F. Stewart, eds. (1987). *Adjustment with a human face: Protecting the vulnerable and promoting growth*. Oxford, UK: Oxford University Press.

De Soto, H. (2000). *The mystery of capital: Why capitalism triumphs in the West and fails everywhere else*. New York: Basic Books.

Deininger, K. (2011). 'Challenges posed by the new wave of farmland investments'. *Journal of Peasant Studies* 38 (2): 217–47.

Department for International Development (DfID) (2013). The New Alliance for Food Security and Nutrition – Ghana Cooperation Framework. Available at: https://www.gov.uk/government/publications/the-new-alliance-for-food-security-and-nutrition-ghana-cooperation-framework. Last accessed: 1 January 2022).

Doss, C. (2006). The effects of intra-household property ownership on expenditure patterns in Ghana. *Journal of African Economies* 15 (1): 149–80.

Duncan, B.A. (2004). *Women in agriculture in Ghana*. Accra, Ghana: Friedrich Ebert Foundation.

Federici, S. (2011). 'Women, land struggles and the reconstruction of the commons'. *Journal of Labor and Society* 14 (1): 41–56.

Ferguson, J. (2006). *Global shadows: Africa in the neoliberal world order*. London: Duke University Press.

Fraser, N. (2009). 'Feminism, capitalism and the cunning of history'. *New Left Review* 56: 97–117.

Friedmann, H. (2005). 'From colonialism to green capitalism: Social movements and the emergence of food regimes'. In Buttel, F.H. and P. McMichael (eds.), *New directions in the sociology of global development*. Amsterdam: Elsevier, pp. 227–64.

Hoogvelt, A. (1997). *Globalization and the post-colonial world: The new political economy of development*. London: Macmillan.

Kassimir, R. (2001). 'Producing local politics: Governance, representation and non-state organisations in Africa'. In Callaghy, T., Kassimir, R. and R. Latham (eds.), *Intervention and transnationalism in Africa: Global-local networks of power*. Cambridge, UK: Cambridge University Press, pp. 93–115.

Lund, C. (2006). 'Twilight institutions: Public authority and local politics in Africa'. *Development and Change* 37 (4): 685–705.

McKeon, N. (2014). *The new alliance for food security and nutrition*. Amsterdam: Transnational Institute.

McMichael, P. (2012). 'The land grab and corporate food regime restructuring'. *Journal of Peasant Studies* 39 (3–4): 681–701.

Peters, P.E. (2009). 'Challenges in land tenure and land reform in Africa: Anthropological contributions'. *World Development* 37 (8): 1317–25.

Platteau, J.P. (1996). 'The evolutionary theory of land rights as applied to sub-Saharan Africa: A critical assessment'. *Development and Change* 27 (1): 29–86.

Prügl, E. (2016). 'Neoliberalism with a feminist face: Crafting a new hegemony at the World Bank'. *Feminist Economics* 23 (1): 30–53.

Quisumbing, A.R. et al. (1995). *Women: The key to food security*. Washington, DC: IFPRI.

Ravnborg, H.M., Spichiger, R., Brandt Broegaard, R. and R. Hundsbaek Pederson (2016). 'Land governance, gender equality and development: Past achievements and remaining challenges'. *Journal of International Development* 28 (3): 412–27.

Razavi, S. (ed.) (2003). *Agrarian change, gender and land rights*. Oxford, UK: Blackwell Publishing.

Reno, W. (1998). *Warlord politics and African states*. Boulder, CO: Lynne Rienner.

Reno, W. (2000). 'Shadow states and the political economy of civil wars'. In Berdal, M. and D.M. Malone (eds.), *Greed and grievance: Economic agendas in civil wars*. Boulder, CO: Lynne Rienner, pp. 43–68.

Rotberg, R.I. (2004). 'The failure and collapse of nation-states: Breakdown, prevention, and repair'. In Rotberg, R.I. (ed.), *When states fail: Causes and consequences*. Princeton, NJ: Princeton University Press, pp. 1–45.

Tsikata, D. and J.A. Yaro (2014). 'When a good business model is not enough'. *Feminist Economics* 20 (1): 202–26.

Van de Walle, N. (2001). *African economics and the politics of permanent crisis*. Cambridge, UK: Cambridge University Press.

Von Braun, J. and R. Meinzen-Dick (2009). *"Land grabbing" by foreign investors in developing countries: Risks and opportunities*. Washington, DC: IFPRI.

Whitehead, A. and D. Tsikata (2003). 'Policy discourses on women's land rights in sub- Saharan Africa: The implications of the re-turn to the customary'. *Journal of Agrarian Change* 3 (1–2): 67–112.

World Bank (2013). *Toolkit for integrating gender-related issues in land policy and administration projects*. Washington, DC: World Bank.

3 Chasing the evolutionary role of chiefs in local land relations

The making and unmaking of chieftaincy in Ghana

Before colonialism, the territory that today makes up Ghana was home to several independent kingdoms, including the large savannah kingdom of Dagomba in the North and a very powerful confederation of Asante states in the centre of the country. Basing their power on the long-established trade of gold and later of slaves with, among others, the Portuguese, who were the first Europeans to arrive in Ghana (1471), the Asante Confederacy had a centralised bureaucratic structure of chieftaincy with the king, the Asantehene, at the top. Other areas (especially northern areas, including today's Volta Region) were characterised by acephalous systems of customary authority, where power (spiritual, judicial and administrative) was divided among different actors, such as Earth Priests (tendamba) or stoolfathers (who usually were in charge of rituals relating to the communities' land), clan heads (related to the first settlers on the land) and family heads (Lentz 2000).

The boundaries between different kingdoms and traditional areas were in flux prior to colonialism, as various wars were fought. Individual land rights were also dynamic, and different resources were subject to complex local rules and regulations; many resources were in fact subjected to a common property regime (at least part of the year), whereas others were privately used but often reverted to common property when left unused. These systems were tightly connected to the local cultural landscape and the fluctuations of local ecosystems (Haller 2010, 2013; Peters 2009). Even though they are sometimes romanticised, these pre-colonial systems of land tenure were by no means egalitarian. Berry (1989, p. 42), for example, highlights how "within descent groups, rights varied according to status – based on seniority, gender, office holding etc.".

DOI: 10.4324/9781003212768-3

Colonial interactions with the "customary" system

After the Portuguese had arrived in Ghana, word of the immense gold reserves in the country quickly spread, and British, Dutch, Swedish and Prussian traders all set up outposts (forts along the coast) in the territory known as the "Gold Coast". The British Gold Coast was established in 1867. In order to consolidate their power over the Gold Coast and to derive benefits from the booming cocoa industry, the British struck a compromise with traditional leaders (Berry 2013, p. 37). As part of the policy of indirect rule, it was decided that the colonial administration would not administer land directly but that it needed to create clear boundaries controlled by a respected authority in order to allocate concessions to European mining and logging companies. An in-depth survey recorded different boundaries as well as different ranks of chieftaincy.

> The extent of the alteration of land rights occurring in this process was not acknowledged: this exercise of fixation and codification was presented as a mere continuation of pre-colonial custom. A close look at the context and motive of the demarcation indicate that the evocation of tradition was, from the start, a strategic and rhetorical mystification. Chiefs understood readily that land titles were a source of quick cash and thus began to decipher colonial procedures for the allocation of prerogatives over soil.
>
> Convincing "traditional" histories – for the canons of British administration – were formulated and presented in front of colonial officials to justify requests for expansion or territorial prerogatives, as well as petitions for elevation of the stools rank.
>
> (Boni 2008, p. 90)

In 1930, the British established native authorities, recognising what they called "precolonial political jurisdictions" and centralising power in Paramount Chieftaincies, who were said to have the "allodial title" or "ultimate title" over land, which reinforced their authority to manage and allocate land and also to collect land tributes from strangers wishing to cultivate stool land. Native authorities hence were given extensive powers of taxation and their claims to land were enshrined in law. Furthermore, Native Tribunals were made mandatory courts of first instance (Boone 2003, pp. 147–48). Native Courts were set up as a part of the British hierarchy of state courts, which meant that "customary laws" applied by Native Courts could become "judicially recognized" and pleaded in state courts as part of the common law of the country (Crook 2008, p. 138).

As colonial powers did in countries all over Africa, the colonial government in Ghana strengthened the power of some chiefs and other selected traditional leaders while eliminating the powers of other traditionally powerful actors (Mamdani 1996). Furthermore, peasants were denied full and secure rights to the land and acknowledged to have only use rights as "subjects" of their respective chief (Boni 2008). Land use rights, however, were embedded in hierarchical descent-based groups, and "insider-outsider distinctions" were made particularly salient and settlers often were considered "politically subordinate" within communities (Boone 2015).

Post-colonial interactions between the state and chiefs

When Kwame Nkrumah, an active leader in the resistance against colonial rule, led the country to independence in 1957, he changed the country's name from Gold Coast to Ghana. Although Nkrumah generally tried to dismantle the vast powers that had been given to chiefs by the colonial government, he did not hesitate to promote those chiefs, who were sympathetic to him and his Convention Peoples Party (CPP), and to ally with them against his opponents (Boone 2003).

In 1962, Nkrumah passed the State Lands Act, which declared that the president had the right to expropriate land from chiefs if it were in the public interest. This measure was meant both to further the cause of state-led industrial agriculture and to weaken the power of chiefs. Although it was left undefined what constitutes the "public interest", large swaths of land were expropriated through compulsory acquisition by the state for the development of state farms, the majority for the planting of industrial crops, such as sugar, palm oil, rubber and cotton. Not only was the objective of replacing small-scale food production with large-scale mechanised farming unachieved (as most food continued to be produced by small-scale farmers), but chiefs also heavily resisted the expropriation of their lands (Amanor 1999). Nkrumah ultimately "failed to uproot chiefly authority and prerogative at the micro-level, where it remained embedded in relations of production and land access and in deeply personalized structures of obligation, dependency and authority" (Boone 2003, p. 177).

Consequent governments continued in their vision to promote large-scale commercial agriculture, in the context of further expropriating large tracts of land from chiefs, leading to widespread and heavy resistance (see Chapter 2). In order to further enable foreign investment and overcome some of the shortcomings of the existing land registry system, the Land Title Registration Law was introduced in

1986 as part of Ghana's structural adjustment package (Spichiger and Stacey 2014). The law was designed to introduce a scheme for registering all interests in land, including those held by stools, skins or lineage groups[1]. According to the Land Title Registration Law, chiefs and other lineage heads were supposed to register their group right (allodial title) without providing names of members of the group. Other interests in land that could be registered:

- **Customary freehold** is community land interest held by subgroups or individuals. Interest is inheritable and holders have the rights to sell, lease, mortgage or pledge their title as long as they recognise the superior authority of the chief.
- **Common-law freehold** can be acquired through a grant made by the allodial owner, either by sale or by gift. This grant requires the parties to agree that their obligations and rights will be regulated by common law.
- **Leasehold rights** allow a person to occupy land for a certain period of time. They can be granted by the allodial freeholder or by the individual holding land under customary freehold.
- **Lesser interest** in land is not properly defined.

Democratisation, decentralisation and the "policy of non-interference in chieftaincy affairs"

As a response to increasing demands from international donors, Ghana's first presidential and multiparty elections were held in 1992. Rawlings won the elections and stayed in power until 2000. Although Rawlings's relations with traditional authorities were initially characterised by mutual distrust, a marked change took place when decentralisation and democratisation policies were pushed forward by international donors, which increased the bargaining power of local authorities (Nyendu 2006). The 1992 Constitution and consequent laws thus also document a shift in the dynamic relationship between customary authorities and the state (Ray 1996).

The 1992 Constitution forms the basis of the current system of decentralisation and sets up District Assemblies (DAs) as the highest political authorities in the districts. District Chief Executives (DCEs) are appointed directly by the President. Although each electoral area elects one member to the DA, a maximum of 30% of the seats are reserved for people directly appointed by the President in consultation with traditional authorities and interest groups in the district (Art. 242). Apart of the formal state structures, the Constitution also formally recognises chieftaincy and customary law: Art. 270 (1) states "The institution of chieftaincy together with its traditional councils as established by customary law and usage is hereby guaranteed". It further defines customary law to be part of the common law of the country (Art. 11, 2–3) and created a National House of Chiefs as well as a Regional House of Chiefs in each region and aimed to codify customary law and abolish harmful customary practices (Art. 271). Currently, 190 government-recognised traditional councils are represented in the House of Chiefs – and most of them date back to the times of colonialism. Traditional Councils are headed by Paramount Chiefs, who have jurisdiction over the whole traditional area and act as presidents of traditional councils (Stacey 2015, p. 34). New chiefs are appointed by traditional councils according to their lineage. They need to swear allegiance to the traditional council before being granted government recognition (Brobbey 2008). The 2008 Chieftaincy Act (Section 15) furthermore declares that the government has no jurisdiction over chieftaincy disputes. The country thus officially recognises two legal fora for dispute settlement: (1) the judiciary made up of superior courts, regional tribunals and lower courts and (2) the traditional courts, which are usually the first point of contact for minor crimes and land conflicts.

The Constitution and consequent legal acts thus firmly established the "hands off approach" (Ray 1996, p. 190) or "policy of non-interference" (Ubink and Quan 2008) of the Ghanaian government towards chieftaincy, which has continued under Rawlings's successors. Although chiefs are not supposed to be politically active on the national level (Constitution, Art. 276 (1)), they nevertheless constitute a powerful political lobby group. Many chiefs serve in national statutory bodies and some have even served as ministers of state (Lavers and Boamah 2016). At the same time, there is an increased tendency to fill chieftaincy positions with highly educated professionals, who often work in close collaboration with the government, leading to a blurring of the division between state professionals and chiefs (Amanor 2008; Boamah 2014). Customary authorities also have substantial influence within the areas of their jurisdiction and their opinions carry a lot of weight at election times[2].

Current land tenure: the statutory and the customary land tenure system

The Ghanaian Constitution distinguishes between public land and stool lands, which are estimated to make up 20% and 80% respectively of the land surface (Kasanga and Kotey 2001). Public land consists of all land that has been acquired by the government in the public interest, including lands vested in the State before the 1992 Constitution was passed. In addition to the Lands Commission, which was established by the Constitution, there are six public land sector agencies with different but sometimes overlapping roles and responsibilities. The large number of land agencies at the national, regional and district level, their overlapping mandates, budgetary and staff constraints and crucially contradictions with local customary rules have made policy implementation difficult (see, for example, Ubink and Quan 2008), and most people continue to derive their access to land primarily through customary institutions. Furthermore, according to the World Bank, only about 30,000 out of an estimated 6 million land parcels in Ghana have been registered at the Land Registry (in line with the 1986 Land Title Registration Act), mainly in Accra and Kumasi. Several "lesser interests in land" were registered without clarifying the allodial title of stools or families, thus leading to countless land disputes (Kasanga and Kotey 2001).

Although the Constitution and subsequent legal acts contain several provisions, which try to limit chiefs' authority, various authors have highlighted that these provisions have largely been ineffective because of budget and staff constraints, pervasive corruption and opposition by customary authorities (Ubink and Quan 2008; Yeboah and Shaw 2013). The Constitution, for example, stipulated that there shall be

> no disposition or development of any stool land unless the Regional Lands Commission of the region in which the land is situated has certified that the disposition or development is consistent with the development plan drawn up or approved by the planning authority for the area concerned.
>
> (Art. 267)

However, a study by Yeboah and Shaw (2013) found that 80% of all developments in Ghana proceed without authorisation from the relevant planning authorities.

The changing face of customary land tenure

Customary land ownership in Ghana relies heavily on narratives around ancestry, tradition and historical events, which serve to continuously re-establish the primordial rights of the groups related to the first settlers on the land (Lentz 2006). Unlike most other areas in Ghana, where chiefs hold the allodial title in land and thus execute judicial, governance and land management functions, land in most of the Volta Region is held by families or clans, who are represented by their family/clan heads. Chiefs in great parts of the Volta Region thus hold only ritual, judicial and functional powers as the heads of their communities but do not have the land management and governance functions associated with stools and skins in other areas (Tsikata 2012).

The land rights of families are strongly linked to their membership to a particular stool, skin or clan, and land rights of individuals are embedded in their membership in a particular family. As such, land rights are "socially and politically embedded" (Lentz 2006, p. 1). Within these systems, families and individuals have rights over individual parcels of land, which are inherited through the male or female line, depending on the inheritance system. Individual parcels can be leased out to other families within the same community. Strangers who wish to acquire land, however, first have to seek the permission of chiefs or family heads (Kasanga and Kotey 2001, p. 13). Since customary systems of land tenure lack maps, cadasters or titles, land rights, sales and leases often are not recorded and individual land rights need continual re-enactment through negotiation and investment in social networks. Amanor also (2008) shows that in many Ghanaian farming systems, where land is not yet scarce, individual farming rights are adapted to a system of shifting cultivation whereby farming plots are flexible in terms of both size and location.

Customary systems embody vast power differentials, particularly related to migration background and gender (Whitehead and Tsikata 2003). Migrant settlers generally do not have the same rights to land as those belonging to native stool, clan or skin groups. Although they may have been granted use rights over land by the respective authority decades (and sometimes even centuries) ago, their rights can be easily re-appropriated by the native group. This makes settlers particularly vulnerable, as land is becoming scarcer and more commodified (Boamah 2014).

Women's land rights are also vulnerable under customary land tenure. Whereas, where land is abundant, male individuals can generally access new land through clearing – an explicitly male task – women have to rely on their husbands and fathers for access to land. Women rarely have control over the allocation of land, which is carried out by chiefs, male lineage heads and household heads. When women are allocated land, it is often a relatively smaller and qualitatively worse plot as compared with men's plots (Whitehead and Tsikata 2003). Particularly in patrilineal societies, which prevail in the Volta Region, women often lose access to their father's land once they get married, especially if they marry into another clan (exogamy). Once married, women are obliged to help their husbands with the cultivation of their plots, often in addition to their own farming activities (Duncan 2004). Upon divorce or death of their husband, widows' continued access to land depends on the husband's family, and childless widows are frequently chased off their land.

People whose land rights have been infringed have a number of options: district or magistrate courts are the lowest-level courts applying formal state law. Although these formal courts often are inaccessible to local people because of high costs involved, around 110 districts also offer alternative dispute resolution or mediation services by the Commission on Human Rights and Administrative Justice. Most people, however, choose to solve land-related disputes locally through family heads, village elders and chiefs and use state courts only as the last option when traditional mechanisms have failed (Spichiger and Stacey 2014). Traditional mechanisms of conflict management rely on elders to mediate in the process of conflict resolution as well as on the power of ancestors and local gods and shrines. Women, youth and settlers usually are not represented within the council of elders, thus making their access to justice dependent on the goodwill of the elders.

Increasing commodification of land and its impacts

Even though, according to the Constitution, stool land cannot be sold, it has been widely acknowledged that in many regions land markets have developed (Ubink and Quan 2008). These often operate without formal documentation and so land purchases are contested in many cases. Researchers have shown that "the social embeddedness of vernacular land markets means that those with greatest influence over land under customary tenure (tribal chiefs and heads of patrilineages) will be best placed to gain from the commoditization of land through rents and sales" (Chimhowu and Woodhouse 2006, p. 360). Although the 1992 Constitution establishes chiefs as the custodians of stool land, who hold the land in trust for their subjects and future generations, it has been documented that, as the value of land is rising, chiefs increasingly pose as the owners of land, in some cases even selling the same parcels of land several times (Ubink and Quan 2008). According to the World Bank (2013, p. 3), "this process of enrichment is facilitated by the influence that chiefs wield over the elected government".

These sales automatically give rise to disputes, as they are often based on oral agreements rather than on written contracts. In the context of unclear land boundaries and embedded land rights, the question also arises "which rights have been transferred: rights to use, to administer, or to further transfer the land, definitely or temporarily, only within one's own lineage or to third parties, for free or in exchange for goods and services etc." (Lentz 2006, p. 23). All over Ghana, there are countless disputes between different stools, skins, clans and families as groups vie for the same piece of land. Although most customary authorities legitimate their claims by referring to their status as first-comers or first settlers on the land, this status and the relative chronology of the history of settlement or the specific boundaries of the land were frequently challenged (Lentz 2006, p. 9).

Integrating customary and statutory land tenure: the Land Administration Project

Because the 1986 Land Title Registration Law had little effect, in 1999 for the first time a comprehensive National Land Policy (revised in 2002) was passed with the aim to strengthen the Land Title Registration Law. It outlines the importance of reducing and eliminating drawn-out land conflicts and boundary disputes and ensures the full participation of traditional authorities and customary landowners in the registration of land titles of different types of landholders. An assessment by the World Bank (2013, p. 4) found that "like the 1992 Constitution before it, the National Land Policy bowed to the chiefs while ostensibly aiming at the same time to introduce more order and transparency in the administration of land".

The Land Administration Project (LAP), a land reform led by the Ministry of Lands and Natural Resources, is based on the National Land Policy. The project, which is funded by a consortium of development agencies (including the United States Agency for International Development and the World Bank), aims "to undertake land policy and institutional reform and key land administration pilots for laying the foundation for a sustainable decentralized land administration system that is fair, efficient, cost effective and ensures land tenure security" (World Bank 2008, p. 12). The project started in 2003 with several pilot projects and is supposed to last 20 years (Spichiger and Stacey 2014). In line with the international policy shift from registering individual land rights to strengthening customary land rights, the LAP builds on customary land tenure systems by officially vesting control over land management, registration and dispute settlement into Customary Land Secretariats (CLSs), which are headed by Paramount Chiefs or by clan or family heads. The CLSs are supposed to work in close collaboration with DAs and the Regional Lands Commission and "serve as an interface between the landowning communities and the public land sector agencies" (Government of Ghana Official Portal, last accessed: 25 April 2018). Land boundaries of traditional areas, as well as individual land rights within these areas, are supposed to be mapped and registered at the Regional Lands Commission in order to increase tenure security for local landholders (Amanor and Ubink 2008). Any interest in land or land transaction first needs to be validated by the respective CLS before being registered in the Regional Lands Commission.

Up until 2016, the LAP undertook some institutional reforms and engaged in pilots for customary boundary demarcation, the establishment of CLS and digitalisation of land records as well as the setting-up of land courts and systematic title registration. It also developed a gender strategy. By 2015, 47 CLSs had been established by traditional authorities with support from the government. The majority of these were set up in regions where chiefs traditionally are in control of land allocation. In the Volta Region, where clans and families hold most of the land, only three CLSs were created, Fievie – the case study described in this book – being one of them (Abdul Karim 2015).

The LAP can be seen as an attempt to formalise the customary sector. It has been criticised by many for being based on a simplified version of customary realities, ignoring local-level power structures (Whitehead and Tsikata 2003), as well as for endorsing the role of chiefs as administrators of land, as if it were a timeless principle. Critics fear that this process will further increase the power of chiefs to shape customary institutions in their own interest at the expense of local smallholder farmers (Ubink and Quan 2008, p. 205). The first studies on the effectiveness of the LAP show that chiefs often use CLSs "for centralizing the management of land transactions and the recording and formal documentation of land rights – as instruments for land disposals by the elite by concentrating on facilitating and documenting new land transactions, and failing to document the rights of indigenous landholders" (Ubink and Quan 2008, p. 208). Furthermore, in a number of locations, local land users have questioned the legitimacy of the government-approved customary authorities that form CLSs (Stacey 2015). The fact that through the LAP CLSs now have to validate all land sales and title registrations may also work against the rural poor, women, pastoralists and especially settlers, who will not be able to register any claims unless they have good relations with the customary authorities.

Even the World Bank evaluation of the project is highly critical, acknowledging the discrepancy between aspiration and reality: "The project endorsed the support for the customary authorities' control of land that was embedded in the 1992 Constitution and the 1999 Land

Policy" and it "also aimed to strengthen the land sector agencies, thereby increasing the state's control over land administration, and shifting rents away from the chiefs". The evaluation came to the conclusion that

> this tension at the heart of the project's design was not resolved during implementation. The net effect was to leave the chief's control over land unchallenged, an outcome that may, on balance, have reduced tenure security for many land users, particularly in those parts of Ghana where the traditional authorities were seeking to profit from rising land values.
>
> (World Bank 2013, p. 16)

The changing face of chieftaincy in the study area

The South Tongu District is located in Ghana's Volta Region, which hosts Lake Volta – one of the world's largest artificial bodies of water and home to Ghana's hydroelectric Akosombo Dam, which provides both Ghana and its neighbouring countries with electricity. Tongu is an Ewe word meaning "along the river", a reference to the fact that the district is stretched out along both sides of the Volta River. Five traditional areas are located partly in the South Tongu District (Tefle, Sokpoe, Fievie, Vume and Agave) and each of them has its own "customary" administrative structures. The Global Agri-Development Company (GADCO) investment is located mainly in the Fievie Traditional Area, which is home to three of the four study communities (Fievie-Dugame, Kpodzi and Kpevikpo) (see Map 3.1). At the time of research, a court case was ongoing to decide whether Bakpa Adzani – the fourth study community, which had been resettled to the area after the establishment of the Akosombo Dam in the 1960s – belonged to the Fievie Traditional Area or the neighbouring Mafi Traditional Area (located in the Central Tongu District).

History and political structure of the Fievie Traditional Area

The Ewe people, who nowadays are found mainly in Ghana's Volta Region, in Togo and in Western Benin, originate from Ketu, a Yoruba town in what is now Benin. As the Yorubas expanded their territory, the Ewes were pushed westward and ended up living in Notsie, where they were ruled by a king. According to oral history, when King Agorkoli ascended the throne, his tyrannical rule forced the Ewe to migrate again in the early 17th century – this time to settle in what is now South-Eastern Ghana and Southern Togo (Amenumey 1986).

Map 3.1 The study area and the four study communities.

Although various groups claim to have been the first settlers in the Volta Region (see Nugent 2010), the Fievie people made a similar claim. According to various chiefs, they were the first to settle down in the area, even before the larger waves of Ewe migrants from Notsie arrived. This is an important strategy, as according to customary law, the first settlers on the land are its owners. Fievie chiefs also used this claim in the various land litigation cases in which they were involved at the time of research.

According to the elders, the Fievie people travelled for over 40 years before settling down at their current location. Detailed stories were told about the various wars that were fought, about the waves of refugees and migrants who were taken in by the Fievies and about the important places in the community, which still hold names of these significant events. Various respondents mentioned that, prior to colonisation, the Fievie people did not have a Paramount Chief but rather revered as their spiritual leader the hunter Akalo, who led them to their current location. He and his five brothers were revered as the founding fathers of Fievie, and the youngest brother, Togbui Amagahadze, was said to be the Stoolfather (Zikpuitor) (i.e. the custodian of the land), as he was the first one who was born in the new location. Other important individuals at the time were the warlords (Awadada) and Mariama, the mother of the six brothers and a warrior herself. At the time of research, there was still a big shrine in Fievie-Dugame, the seat of the chieftaincy, where Akalo was said to have disappeared. As some of the brothers got married, the Fievie population grew and four clans (Amegafeme, Afegame, Afevieme and Awagafeme) established their lineages (also called gates).

Colonisation

Between 1884 and 1914, most of Eweland was colonised by the Germans and called German Togoland. This era of German colonialism was characterised by the "exaction of compulsory labor, the imposition of a host of direct taxes, restriction of the freedom of the people to trade, infringement of their right to the land and a curtailment of the power of the chiefs" (Amenumey 1969, p. 636). In 1918, as Germany lost World War I, a League of Nations mandate divided German colonies between France, Great Britain and Belgium. Roughly one third of German Togoland thus was integrated into the British Gold Coast, and two thirds were given to the French and later became Togo (Laumann 2003).

Whereas the Germans had attempted to curtail the power of single big chiefs by giving autonomy to every individual chief and subchief to establish their own tribunal, the British had another policy. At the onset of the integration of the Ewe territories into the British Gold Coast, there were 243 independent tribunals (Yayoh 2013). This proved to be a problem for the British strategy of indirect rule. Unlike in other Gold Coast territories, there were no "big chiefs" who could serve the interests of the colonial masters. So the colonial government sought to restructure the whole territory by integrating various fragmented states into bigger entities headed by Paramount Chiefs for the purpose of indirect rule. This policy of amalgamation, which saw the integration of relatively small settlements (dukowo) ranging from 100 to 5000 people into larger hierarchical states (more than 15,000 people), formed the core of the British indirect rule in the Volta Region. This endeavour vastly increased the power of some chiefs, reduced that of others and consequently was met with much resistance and the eruption of many chieftaincy disputes, as Subdivisional Chiefs struggled to become Divisional Chiefs and Divisional Chiefs attempted to become Paramount Chiefs (Yayoh 2013, p. 245).

Generally, traditional areas came to be organised around a Paramount Chief (Fiãga), sometimes referred to as King; the various clan heads, referred to as Divisional Chiefs (Dufiawo); and several subchiefs and village heads (Sãmefiawo). All male chiefs tended to be addressed as "togbui" (meaning grandfather or ancestor), and female chiefs as "mama" (mother). Both the Paramount Chief and their sub-chiefs usually had a Queen Mother (Nyonufia, literally "women's chief"), who had to come from the same clan as the respective chief. Queen Mothers in most of the Volta Region, however, wielded much less power than in other regions, especially Akan areas of Ghana (see Nyendu 2006, p. 9).

Many Paramount Chiefs as well as all Divisional Chiefs also had a Stoolfather (Zikpuitor), who had to be part of the family of the Paramount Chief and acted as the symbolic father of the chief and as custodian of the land. The Paramount Stoolfather often was in charge of enstooling all chiefs. The process of enstooling involved certain rituals (such as the slaughtering of animals) and the handing over of the symbolic wooden stool to the chief (the stool is supposed to be animated by the spirits of the ancestors). Furthermore, the Paramount Chief, the Paramount Queen Mother and the Divisional Chiefs each had a linguist (tsiami) who spoke for them on public occasions. The Paramount Chief, his Stoolfather and the Divisional Chiefs and their Stoolfathers, as well as the War Leaders (Awadada), formed the Traditional Council, which needed to be consulted for any decision. Various traditions thus were kept alive under colonialism and even survive to this day, and others were added and modified to adapt the chieftaincy system to the changed socioeconomic context.

Colonisation changed the structure of leadership in the Fievie Traditional Area, where – according to numerous respondents – all important positions (Paramount Chief, Paramount Stoolfather and Paramount Queen Mother) initially were taken by the lineage of the first Paramount Stoolfather (Amegafeme[3]), who asserted his power through references to historical events.

And for instance, my gate was the Stoolfather gate but at a point, there was a war at Fievie and all the other gates fled. (…) So, they went back to some other communities and places but it was only my gate that stayed, there was one man in our gate, the leader of one of the shrines. The shrine asked the leader not to leave, so he stayed on. Because he stayed on through the war and after the war, it was like all the powers, all the properties and all other things were under his control. So, when even after the war the other people came, you know that he has already taken possession of all the things, you cannot come back to take the things. That was how all the things shifted to our gate.

(E19, local Queen Mother in the Fievie Traditional Area, Fievie-Dugame, 25 June 2016)

However, when the last Paramount Chief passed away, no suitable man from his clan could be found to fill his position. Therefore, the Paramount Stoolfather at the time decided to enstool a Paramount Chief from another clan (Afegame). This created some major division within the Fievie Chieftaincy, which also became evident when GADCO arrived in the area, as will be highlighted in Chapter 4.

Although chiefs in the Volta Region did not have the vast land management functions associated with chiefs in other areas of Ghana, they were in charge of enforcing customary rules and regulations for communally used lands and of settling any land-related disputes. They furthermore held important symbolic, ritual and organisational functions in the communities and were also in charge of dispute resolution. Chiefs symbolised the identity of their communities, as they directly represented the collective ancestors and kept traditions alive.

They were also in charge of organising communal labour and medical aid in emergency situations (see Kainz 2012, p. 40). Chiefs thus held very important positions in their communities, and people generally did not criticise their chiefs (especially not in public), as they were seen to be the direct representatives of the ancestors and thus always thought to be acting for the benefit of the whole community. Anybody wishing to have a personal audience with a chief in order to discuss a personal problem and ask for assistance traditionally needed to present a bottle of Schnapps to the chief, as a way to acknowledge his help – a practice that was still necessary in order to conduct research in the different villages.

Even though chiefs were generally held in very high esteem, they were very much dependent on the goodwill of their communities and especially the youth (which comprised all men roughly below the age of 60). If the youth were dissatisfied with one of their chiefs, they had the possibility of destooling him – a procedure which entailed all youth going together to the respective chief's house and seizing his stool, thus demonstrating that they were no longer under his authority.

Current political structure of the Fievie Traditional Area

At the time of research, the Fievie Traditional Area was still headed by the Paramount Chief from the Afegame gate, while rather than and? the Paramount Stoolfather and the Paramount Queen Mother came from Amegafeme gate. Both the Paramount Chief and his Stoolfather were highly educated (both PhD holders) and resided not in the local area but predominantly in Accra. The Paramount Queen Mother lived in Fievie-Dugame, the seat of the chieftaincy. On several occasions, she mentioned that she was often left out of important decisions regarding the Fievie Traditional Area, as these tended to be taken by men. The four clan heads or Divisional Chiefs with their respective Stoolfathers and the war leaders (Awadada) of the Fievie State made up the Traditional Council of the Paramountcy, which was supposed to be consulted before any major decisions were taken.

The Traditional Area was made up of 57 villages, most of which were headed by a village chief or village head (53 in total) who was in charge of organising village life, settling minor land and other disputes within the village as well as fostering general developments at the village level. Furthermore, most villages had Queen Mothers, Youth Chiefs, War Chiefs (or warriors) and linguists. The role of Queen Mothers was generally confined to organising women for communal labour and settling disputes between women, and Youth Chiefs were in charge of organising the youth (sohewo), which comprised all men roughly below the age of 60. War leaders in turn had more symbolic functions; that is, in case of a war between different traditional areas, they were supposed to lead the men to war.

Regular community meetings were held in the traditional area in order to discuss any problems or issues and to pass on important messages from the government or the National or Regional House of Chiefs to the community. In order to announce these meetings, each community had a "gongo" (drum) beater, who walked around the village with a drum. Notably, the meetings I attended were frequented mainly by middle-aged and elderly people. Furthermore, even though many women were present, only a few (mostly elderly and influential) women dared to speak.

The history of the Fievie Traditional Area remained very important in day-to-day life, and references to historical events were continually used to (re)establish chiefly authority as well as authority over land, as will be shown in the following chapters. Every year, in order to celebrate the unity and strength of the Fievie Traditional Area, the Fievie people held a large homecoming ceremony to honour their ancestors and the events that led them to arrive at their current location.

Settlers in the Fievie Traditional Area

Two of the study villages – Kpodzi and Kpevikpo – were established by settlers from the Tefle Traditional Area prior to colonisation. However, at the time of research, the communities had become integrated in the Fievie Traditional Area, as there had been significant intermarriage with Fievie citizens and several Fievie people also had moved to these settlements. Even though the descendants of the original settlers were still considered settlers in terms of land ownership, they were part of the Fievie community in terms of participation in community meetings or communal labour.

The fourth study area village – Bakpa Adzani – was established in the 1960s as a result of the construction of the Akosombo Dam and the consequent flooding of various communities in the North Tongu District. The resettled communities still pledged allegiance to the Bakpa Traditional Area, which similar to the Fievie Traditional Area, had its own founding myths and history celebrated annually in a festival called "Klokpoza" (from the name of Klokpo in Nigeria, where Bakpa people originated from). The Bakpa Traditional Area was structured along similar lines as the Fievie Traditional Area. The whole traditional area covered 37 villages and was headed by a Paramount Chief, his Secretary, clan heads or Divisional Chiefs of the eight clans as well as by several subchiefs and Queen Mothers. Although several Bakpa communities were still located in North Tongu, Bakpa Adzani and New Bakpa, which held the seat of the Paramountcy, had been resettled to the South Tongu District. Even though some intermarriage also took place between Fievie citizens and Bakpas, Bakpa people, unlike the cattle rearers of Kpodzi and Kpevikpo, were not recognised as citizens of the Fievie Traditional Area and therefore were not included in any important decisions or community meetings relating to the Fievie Traditional Area. The land rights of both groups of settlers were precarious.

Customary land tenure

All land in the Fievie Traditional Area was vested in the four Fievie clans and "owned" by families within these clans. Each of the clans was made up of about 8 to 10 families. Family land was under the control of the male family heads (usually the oldest man in the family), who exercised most of the rights usually associated with property ownership. They allocated land to individual family members and made broader land management decisions. They could also provide any unused family land to other villagers as gifts or leases or for sharecropping.

Traditionally, customary authorities or clan heads could not give out land without consulting the relevant family heads, but at the time of research, family heads were increasingly selling land.

Individual family members held only use rights over their piece of land. If they stopped farming their land, it could be re-allocated to another person or be assigned for another use by the family head. Any member of the Fievie Traditional Area could enter the land, if left fallow, for cattle grazing purposes or cutting of firewood, but the overall authority remained with the family head. Even though there were no obvious boundary demarcations, individuals generally knew which land belonged to which family. Minor land disputes between families usually were settled at the village level through customary means.

Although individual users could statutorily register their land with the Regional Lands Commission, hardly anybody had done so at the time of research.

Formally, very few, I am even told just about 10% went ahead to register their land statutorily. They get a receipt from land owners and they think that is enough and they can use it for as long as they want but because land is getting scarcer and scarcer, people are having to learn from that and getting it registered.

(E5a, DCE, Sogakope, 22 May 2014)

The reasons for this negligence were manifold. On the one hand, the cost of land registration was too high for most people. On the other hand, an individual land user would need to have the approval of the family head in order to go ahead and register land statutorily, and approval depended a great deal on the person's relationship to the family head and the elders. Since women's land rights were customarily dependent on men, it was even more difficult for a woman to receive permission to statutorily register her plot.

Prior to the arrival of the GADCO, large tracts of land in the Fievie Traditional Area were not under cultivation. Anybody wishing to establish a farm on this land had to approach the responsible family head for permission. A large area of grassland had been allocated to settlers (including Kpodzi and Kpevikpo) for the main purpose of cattle rearing, and rules and regulations for the use of pasture and other common pool resources found on the land were devised by the traditional authorities. Any infringements of the rules would be reported to the traditional authorities and subjected to customary dispute resolution. In that sense, even though the land belonged to a particular family, it was administered by the customary authorities.

The settler communities of Kpodzi and Kpevikpo also used the grazing areas for gardening and small-scale farming, and it was not clear whether each individual had to ask for permission in order to engage in farming after the vast land area had been allocated for the purpose of cattle herding. For the use of other common pool resources, such as fuelwood, thatch or wild fruits, no permission was needed. Although fuelwood could be collected on any uncultivated land, the main rule was that no young trees should be felled for fuelwood. No regulations existed for the use of wild fruits or thatch. It appeared that anybody from within, as well as from outside, the Fievie Traditional Area was allowed to collect fuelwood and thatch from the vast savannah bushlands. In practice, however, it was mostly women from the Fievie Traditional Area, as well as from the two Bakpa communities, who used these common pool resources.

Fishing in the floodplains also underlaid a seasonal regime. Various fishponds were located on the floodplains. These belonged to specific families from within the Fievie Traditional Area whose forefathers had manually dug them. Some of these families owned up to 10 fishponds. Although anybody could catch fish in the floodplains during the rainy season, the use of fishponds reverted to the owners during the dry season. The ponds then could be used by any family member in accordance with the rules established by the family head. The harvest usually was shared among the whole family as well as individual helpers, and the elders were given a specific quota.

Though used by different use groups, the various common pool resources were most important for women, settlers and poor landless people (i.e. for those people whose land rights are most precarious under customary land tenure).

Women's land rights under customary land tenure

Women generally accessed land either through the family head or upon marriage through their husbands. Whereas women who married outside their clan tended to lose access to their fathers' land upon marriage, those marrying within their own clan often continued to have use rights and, in some cases, could also pass on the plots to their children. In the case of women from the important lineage of the Paramount Stoolfather, some men even accessed land through their wives, although this was the exception to the rule.

Once married, most women received a plot of land from their husband, which they cultivated independently (while providing labour on their husband's plots). Generally, their plot was considerably smaller than their husband's, in some cases just a "garden" with food crops for family use. Upon divorce or widowhood, women generally were vulnerable to dispossession, as the husband's family could reclaim their land. Several incidences of such "land grabbing" from widows were reported, and childless women were particularly at risk. Some of these widows were able to revert to their own family's land if plots were still available, and others engaged in sharecropping. Similarly, according to a representative of the

LAP, women in so-called "informal marriages" (co-habitation of unmarried couples) – a practice becoming more and more common all over Ghana – were particularly endangered to being dispossessed from their "husband's" land (E20, LAP Representative, 12 May 2016).

As land was becoming more valuable and scarcer, it was concentrated in the hands of a few families. Whether or not women could have easy access to land depended on the size of the land of their own or their husband's family and on their relationship to the family head and elders.

> Most of the time it depends on power, who has more power. Because we have a few women who have strong power. And it is about buying the love and trust of the elders of the family, where they would talk on your behalf. But if they don't talk on your behalf, you can easily lose your land.
>
> (E7, Director, Women's Empowerment non-governmental organization (NGO), Tefle, 18 July 2014)

Land rights of "settlers"

As shown before, in the Fievie Traditional Area, there were various settler communities, including three of the study communities (Kpodzi, Kpevikpo and Bakpa Adzani). The fact that settlers did not trace their ancestry back to the lineages making up the traditional area made their use rights to land under customary tenure much less secure, especially as land was becoming more and more valuable (see also Stacey 2015).

The leaders of Kpodzi and Kpevikpo – the two communities established by settlers from the Tefle Traditional Area more than 100 years ago for the purpose of cattle rearing – had at the time approached the land-owning family to be allowed to use the land. Initially, the settlers had to pay a yearly levy of one cow per kraal for being allowed to use the grazing land, but many decades ago these payments stopped as settlers became more and more integrated in Fievie society (through intermarriage). They also used the land for farming, and the head of Kpevikpo village managed the land for the village in the knowledge that they were not the owners of the land.

> You have the right to build a house, you have the right to farm, you have the right to fish, you have the right to do any economic activity you want to do. However, if you are a settler, you are not the owner of the place.
>
> (Expert Interview, member of the CLS, Sogakope, 6 February 2015, *DS)

The land rights of the resettled Bakpa communities were even more precarious, as it was not clear whether the land they now occupied was originally provided by the Fievie Traditional Area or by the adjoining Mafi Traditional Area. Whereas Fievie chiefs claimed to have given the land for the resettlement and thus saw Bakpa people as mere "settlers" or "immigrants", Bakpa clans were divided on the matter: some claimed that the land originated from Fievie and others argued that it originated from Mafi. According to a newspaper article published in the *Ghanaian Times* on 6 March 1965, the Divisional Chief of Adidome Togbe Kosinri Agyeman III gave 19,360 acres (about 7800 ha) of the land of the Mafi Traditional Area to the government in order to resettle the flood-affected Bakpa communities. But this is disputed by the Fievie chiefs, who on two occasions leased out large tracts of Bakpa-used farmland to foreign investors, thus claiming ownership of the land.

The role of district authorities

The South Tongu District was one of the first districts to be established (1988). At the time of research, it was headed by the DCE, who was appointed by the President and had to be approved by the assembly members. The South Tongu District Assembly, the highest decision-making body in the district, had a total of 60 members: 40 members were voted in by their respective electoral areas and 20 members were appointed by the President. The majority of higher-level district officials, as well as 39 of the 40 elected local assembly members in 2014, were male. Seven of the appointed members were female (E5a, DCE, Sogakope, 22 May 2014).

The main task of the district authorities was to "see to the general decentralization of government policies from the national level to the local levels, which is done through the various decentralized and other centralized structures" (E5a, DCE, 22 May 2014). So the district was engaged in education, health, planning and agricultural development – the concrete implementation of policies, however, was often made difficult by a lack of funds and staff.

Although the district authorities were supposed to provide infrastructure, such as schools and running water to the communities, they first had to negotiate with the traditional authorities (and responsible family heads) for the allocation of land for these projects. Often, communities also had to provide free labour to help with construction. Generally, the labour was provided either by the youth (organised by the Youth Chief) or by women (organised by the Queen Mother).

At the time of research, large parts of the Fievie Traditional Area had no running water and the households relied mainly on rivers, springs and ponds. Furthermore, most houses in the study communities had no electricity – a result of the district's lack of funds and staff. Many infrastructural, health and agricultural projects in the district thus were funded with the help of international donors and NGOs. In line with the general low capacity of the district, its role in agricultural development and large-scale land acquisitions (LSLAs) was also rather limited.

The role of the district in agricultural development and large-scale agricultural land acquisitions

Agricultural policies were implemented mainly through the District Directorate of Agriculture, and the overall agricultural policy framework provided guidance to its activities (see Chapter 2). At the time of the first field research in 2014, 16 agricultural extension officers were working in the district – they helped with the establishment of farmer groups, offered training to these groups and provided inputs, such as fertilizers, at subsidised prices. However, according to the District Director of Agriculture, they were facing serious financial constraints, which made policy implementation difficult.

Owing to the broader FASDEP (Food and Agriculture Sector Development Project) II policy orientation on attracting foreign investment in agriculture, the District Directorate of Agriculture was also keen to assist investors with inputs and advice (E6, District Director for Agriculture, Sogakope, 16 April 2014). However, as has been highlighted above, all land in the study area was held under customary land tenure, and statutory bodies, such as the Town and Country Planning Unit or the Regional Lands Commission, exercised very limited oversight and control. Most LSLAs thus were negotiated directly between chiefs and foreign investors.

> What is in place is that if an investor or an individual needs land, they hardly go to government for land. They go to the chiefs and land owners. The chiefs show them the lands that are available then they negotiate and then the cost of interest in that land is usually arbitrary. (…) Then they prepare a receipt indicating that they have sold the interest in the piece of land to so and so to be used for so and so purpose. More often than not, people start using the land based on that receipt but statutorily, when you are given the land by the traditional leaders, you need to go to the Lands Commission to get it documented in the national plan.
>
> (E5a, DCE, Sogakope, 22 May 2014)

Various government representatives showcased that by not registering their lease with the Regional Lands Commission, investors ultimately created problems for themselves, as leases often became the subject of disputes between different traditional authorities.

Furthermore, any investor leasing over 40 ha would have to get permission from the DA and contact the Environmental Protection Agency (EPA) (located in Ho, the capital of the Volta Region) and with their help undertake an Environmental Impact Assessment. Again, according to various government officials, this hardly ever took place, mainly because of weak enforcement or monitoring from the EPA. According to the DCE, investors and traditional authorities often started involving the government authorities only once there were problems or conflicts over the land, in which case the district frequently took on a mediating function, trying to resolve disputes. This was also the case with conflicts created by the GADCO LSLA, as will be described in the following chapters.

Interactions between government and traditional authorities

Although government officials were frequently left out of negotiating land acquisitions, there were regular interactions between chiefs and government officials on other matters, such as infrastructural developments or health issues. Several of the chiefs interviewed confirmed that they regularly visited the DA and passed on important messages from the community to the assembly and vice versa. According to the District Development Officer, however, the DA generally catered to the traditional authorities and not the other way round.

> As far as I know the traditional authorities, in the first place we cater for them. (…) All that I can say is that the collaboration is there; they come as and when they have any issue for the Assembly to address, then they would come to the Assembly for resolution or whatever.
> (E27, District Planning Officer, Sogakope, 5 July 2016)

It was very evident that many traditional authorities in the Fievie Traditional Area, as in other areas of Ghana (see, for example, Amanor 2008), were highly educated professionals who had a number of close connections to the government elite. Both the Paramount Chief and the Paramount Stoolfather were PhD holders – the Paramount Chief had served as a Deputy Clerk to the Ghanaian Parliament (Nyendu 2006), the Stoolfather's brother had a high position at the Ministry of

Finance and another clan head had previously worked for the Ghana Lands Commission. Nyendu (2006, pp. 363–64) also found that, between 1988 and 2006, 21 out of a total of 68 government appointees to the DAs had been traditional authorities, mostly supporters of the President's party.

Furthermore, during various informal conversations, people complained that "chiefs were being pulled into politics through the back door", as, in order to campaign in a certain area, politicians needed to visit the chiefs and present them with a bottle of Schnapps to get their blessing. So, apparently, chiefs were frequently bribed to support a specific politician (Research Diary 1, 16 Mary 2014, 13 June 2014). After the finalisation of the field research, newly elected President Nana Akufo-Addo appointed a new DCE, who happened to be the brother of the Paramount Chief of the Fievie Traditional Area. These close connections between chiefs and the central government served to strengthen the bargaining power of some chiefs in the context of LSLAs, as will be shown in Chapter 4.

Most individuals continued to be more connected to the chieftaincy system than to the government system, as there were regular community meetings organised by the traditional authorities and various rituals and ceremonies contributed to maintain strong ties with them. As will be highlighted in the discussion of the GADCO investment, customary authorities usually were the first point of contact for many people. Statutory authorities were evoked only when customary means of dispute settlement or negotiation failed. However, owing to the close connections between the customary authorities and the state, these petitions often were not successful (see Chapter 5). The establishment of a CLS in the Fievie Traditional Area further integrated the statutory and the customary systems of land tenure and served to strengthen the bargaining power of chiefs in the local area to the extent that the whole land tenure system was slowly changed.

Integrating the statutory and the customary sector through the creation of a Customary Land Secretariat

As part of the LAP, a CLS was established in the Fievie Traditional Area in 2008. In 2015, it was one of only three in the Volta Region since most of the Secretariats had been established in stool land areas, where chiefs had centralised control over land (Abdul Karim 2015). Through the CLS, a Land Management Committee was established. This included the Paramount Chief, the Paramount Stoolfather, the four clan heads, an accountant, a lawyer and a representative of the

DA. Some women were included in the Land Management Committee and there was even a female chairman (a local Queen Mother from the clan of the Paramount Stoolfather). All of these women were highly educated and part of the customary elite. Through the CLS, Fievie customary authorities had registered the land of the Fievie State at the Regional Lands Commission. Although Secretariats were also supposed to register and map individual land rights within the Fievie State, this had not been done at the time of the research. Rather, the customary authorities used the increased recognition by the Ghanaian state to strengthen their position as "landowners" in the various land litigation cases as well as in the face of increased interest in their land by investors. It actually appeared that they were using the CLS to shift control away from the family heads towards a more centralised land tenure system, as is common in other areas of Ghana.

> They haven't formally told us this, but we go on visits and sometimes we talk to the community and they think that the chief is using the CLS to capture their land. It is like the chief wanted to establish the CLS, so that all the family land would come under the CLS and he will have authority.
>
> (E20, LAP Representative, Accra, 12 May 2016)

On various occasions, members of the CLS mentioned that families were mere "caretakers" of the land and that the allodial title to the land rested with the clan heads and the CLS, who also had the power to divest large tracts of land to third parties and make other major decisions regarding land use. (It was frequently mentioned in interviews that the four clan heads had the "power of attorney" over the land.)

> We have other communities where the land is owned by families, but it is very difficult when it comes to investment. Because let's say, family A is prepared to convey their land, family B may not be willing, family C may be willing, so how do you go about it? So, ours, we have central control over the land, so investors can just come to us. We don't have it anywhere in the country, apart from Ashanti land, we are the only people who have this central ownership.
>
> (E14a, Paramount Stoolfather, Sogakope, 24 May 2014)

This view of changing land tenure in favour of the chiefs was echoed in various informal conversations as well as at the final research dissemination meeting, where a young man got up to shout that their chiefs had taken over all their family lands and that no benefit was coming to them (Fievie-Dugame, 6 July 2016). In this context, the actual "land-owning" families were also increasingly selling land, which could partly be explained by families taking advantage of rising land prices but also as a strategy to prevent the disposition of land by customary authorities. However, through the intervention of the LAP, any land sales are now supposed to be registered in the CLS, where a stamp is put on the transaction to validate the land sale. Only a document with a stamp by the CLS is valid and can be registered in the Regional Lands Commission. Customary authorities also used this statutory formalisation of their role to adapt customary rules and reassert their position as the allodial landholders.

> Under normal circumstances it is only the Fievie state that can convey, because it is a communal land, but that practice is coming under serious threat. People are challenging it. They are selling their land. And you can't be litigating with your citizens, so what we see is that, if a practice is under pressure that practice is calling for a change. So, you have to listen to the people. So, what we do is that, if you want to convey, fine, do it, but come to the community – we have a Secretariat, so we are going to convey the land and give 2/3 to you, then the [Fieve] state takes 1/3. That money we use to manage the state.
>
> (E14a, Paramount Stoolfather, Sogakope, 24 May 2014)

Even though families were selling land to individuals and many were not complying with the above-mentioned rules, all investors were being channelled through the CLS, and according to its chairman, several investors had approached the secretariat for land since its establishment. According to some members of the CLS, lease contracts were negotiated by the Land Management Committee and the four clan heads were said to hold power of attorney over all land in the Fievie Traditional Area. It was clear that, for the Fievie chiefs, LSLAs were also a means to perform and assert their authority over land in the face of competing claims as well as in the various court cases the Traditional Area was involved in (see also Boamah 2014).

> We feel like we have an invincible title over the land, you cannot challenge us. And now we have exercised our right of ownership in several ways. We gave that portion of land to Galten, we gave it as an international lease. So, if it comes to exercising our right of ownership, I think we have done it in a large measure. So, let's see what happens in court.
>
> (E14a, Paramount Stoolfather, Sogakope, 24 May 2014)

The GADCO investment thus took place in a context of rising prices of land and ongoing transformations of the customary system, which through the LAP was increasingly strengthened and legitimised by the state.

Notes

1 The system of customary authority differs across regions in Ghana. In Southern Ghana, chiefs are often called stools, referring to the symbolic wooden stool on which traditional chiefs sit. The word "skin" refers to animal hides, which are the symbols of chiefs' power in Northern Ghana. Tendamba or "earth priests" are the descendants of the first settlers in Northern Ghana. The Volta Region is a special case in Ghana, as most land is held by families or clans, who are represented by their family/clan heads (Kasanga and Kotey 2001). The heads of these groups (such as chiefs, earth-priests or family heads) are said to hold the allodial rights over the land, whereas all members of the group enjoy usufruct rights.
2 In 2012, selected chiefs thus were given brand-new Toyotas by the leading National Democratic Congress (NDC); in 2015 – at the time of research – the NDC government spent USD $37.5 million on Nissan Patrols to be given to chiefs for their support in the 2016 election.
3 Amega means "big man" in Ewe, so the literal meaning of Amegafeme is "house of a big man".

References

Abdul Karim, I. (2015). *An analysis of the customary land secretariat of the land administration project in Ghana.* Cape Coast, Ghana: Institute of Development Studies, University of Cape Coast.

Amanor, K.S. (1999). *Global restructuring and land rights in Ghana: Forest food chains, timber and rural livelihoods.* Uppsala, Sweden: Nordiska Africa Institute.

Amanor, K.S. (2008). 'The changing face of customary land tenure'. In Ubink, J.M. and K.S. Amanor (eds.), *Contesting land and custom in Ghana: State, chief and citizen.* Leiden, The Netherlands: Leiden University Press, pp. 55–81.

Amanor, K.S. and J.M. Ubink (2008). 'Contesting land and custom in Ghana: Introduction'. In Ubink, J.M. and K.S. Amanor (eds.), *Contesting land and custom in Ghana: State, chief and citizen.* Leiden, The Netherlands: Leiden University Press, pp. 9–27.

Amenumey, D. (1969). 'German administration in Southern Togo'. *Journal of African History* 10 (4): 623–39.

Amenumey, D. (1986). *The Ewe in pre-colonial times: A political history with special emphasis on the Anlo, Ge and Krepi.* Accra, Ghana: Sedco Publishing Limited.

Berry, S. (1989). 'Social institutions and access to resources'. *Africa: Journal of the International African Institute* 59 (1): 41–55.

Berry, S. (2013). 'Questions of ownership: Proprietorship and control in a changing rural terrain – A case study from Ghana'. *Africa* 83 (1): 36–56.

Boamah, F. (2014). 'How and why chiefs formalise land use in recent times: The politics of land dispossession through biofuels investments in Ghana'. *Review of African Political Economy* 41 (141): 406–23.

Boni, S. (2008). 'Traditional ambiguities and authoritarian interpretations in Sefwi land disputes'. In Ubink, J.M. and K.S. Amanor (eds.), *Contesting land and custom in Ghana: State, chief and citizen*. Leiden, The Netherlands: Leiden University Press, pp. 81–112.

Boone, C. (2003). 'Decentralization as political strategy in West Africa'. *Comparative Political Studies* 36: 355–80.

Boone, C. (2015). 'Land tenure regimes and state structure in rural Africa: implications for forms of resistance against large-scale land acquisitions by outsiders'. *Journal of Contemporary African Studies* 33 (2): 171–90.

Brobbey, S.A. (2008). *The law of chieftaincy in Ghana*. Accra, Ghana: Advanced Legal Publications.

Chimhowu, A. and P. Woodhouse (2006). 'Customary vs. private property rights? Dynamics and trajectories of vernacular land markets in sub-Saharan Africa'. *Journal of Agrarian Change* 6 (3): 346–71.

Crook, R. (2008). 'Customary justice institutions and local alternative dispute resolution: What kind of protection can they offer to customary landholders?' In Ubink, J.M. and K.S. Amanor (eds.), *Contesting land and custom in Ghana: State, chief and citizen*. Leiden, The Netherlands: Leiden University Press, pp. 55–81.

Duncan, B.A. (2004). *Women in agriculture in Ghana*. Accra, Ghana: Friedrich Ebert Foundation.

Haller, T., ed. (2010). *Disputing the floodplains: Institutional change and the politics of resource management in African floodplains*. Leiden, The Netherlands: Brill.

Haller, T. (2013). *The contested floodplain: Institutional change of the commons in the Kafue Flats, Zambia*. Lanham, MD: Rowman & Littlefield.

Kainz, M. (2012). *At the end of the day, the land belongs to the community: Eine rechtsanthropologische Annäherung an das Verhältnis zwischen der Red Bull Soccer Academy West Africa Ltd. und dem lokalen Umfeld in Ghana*. MA thesis, Vienna: University of Vienna.

Kasanga, R.K. and N.A. Kotey (2001). *Land management in Ghana: Building on tradition and modernity*. London: IIED.

Laumann, D. (2003). 'A historiography of German Togoland, or the rise and fall of a "model colony"'. *History in Africa* 30: 195–211.

Lavers, T. and F. Boamah (2016). 'The impact of agricultural investments on state capacity: A comparative analysis of Ethiopia and Ghana'. *Geoforum* 72: 94–103.

Lentz, C. (2000). '"Chieftaincy has come to stay": Chieftaincy in the acephalous societies of Northwestern Ghana'. *Cahier d'Études Africaines* 40 (159): 593–613.

Lentz, C. (2006). 'Land rights and the politics of belonging in Africa: An introduction'. In Kuba, R. and C. Lentz (eds.), *Land and the politics of belonging in West Africa*. Leiden, The Netherlands: Brill, pp. 1–34.

Mamdani, M. (1996). *Citizen and subject: Contemporary Africa and the legacy of late colonialism*. Princeton, NJ: Princeton University Press.

Nugent, P. (2010). 'The historicity of ethnicity: Mandinka/Joya and Ewe/ Agotime identities in the Nineteenth and Twentieth centuries'. In Keese, A. (ed.), *Ethnicity and the long-term perspective: The African experience*. Bern, Switzerland: Peter Lang.

Nyendu, M. (2006). *Enhancing the participation of traditional authorities (chiefs) in Ghana's democratic decentralization programme: A case study of the South Tongu District Assembly of the Volta Region*. PhD dissertation. Calgary, AB: University of Calgary.

Peters, P.E. (2009). 'Challenges in land tenure and land reform in Africa: Anthropological contributions'. *World Development* 37 (8): 1317–25.

Ray, D.I. (1996). 'Divided sovereignty'. *Journal of Legal Pluralism and Unofficial Law* 28 (37–38): 181–202.

Spichiger, R. and P.A. Stacey (2014). *Ghana's land reform and gender equality*. Copenhagen: Danish Institute for International Studies (DIIS).

Stacey, P. (2015). 'Political structure and the limits of recognition and representation in Ghana'. *Development and Change* 46 (1): 25–47.

Tsikata, D. (2012). *Living in the shadow of the large dam*. Accra, Ghana: Woeli Publishing Services.

Ubink, J.M. and J.F. Quan (2008). 'How to combine tradition and modernity? Regulating customary land management in Ghana'. *Land Use Policy* 25 (2): 198–213.

Whitehead, A. and D. Tsikata (2003). 'Policy discourses on women's land rights in sub- Saharan Africa: The implications of the re-turn to the customary'. *Journal of Agrarian Change* 3 (1–2): 67–112.

World Bank (2008). *Project paper for the restructuring of the Ghana land administration project*. Report no. 45705. Washington, DC: World Bank.

World Bank (2013). *Project performance assessment report Ghana land administration project*. Washington, DC: World Bank.

Yayoh, W.K. (2013). 'Protests against amalgamation in colonial Ewedome, 1920 to 1948'. *Journal of History and Cultures* (2): 1–16.

Yeboah, E. and D.P. Shaw (2013). 'Customary land tenure practices in Ghana: Examining the relationship with land use planning delivery'. *International Development Planning Review* 35 (1): 21–39.

4 Implementation of a land deal in a plural legal setting

The Global Agro-Development Company: a "best practice" large-scale land acquisition

At the time of research, several large-scale land-based investments were located in the study area; all of them had been negotiated between the Fievie customary authorities and the respective investors. In 2007, Red Bull GmbH (of Austria) acquired land from the Fievie Traditional Area to establish a football academy, which was still operational at the time of research. In 2009, Galten, an Israeli Jatropha company, also leased land from the Fievie Traditional Area. This investment had gone bankrupt by the time of the research and an injunction had been placed on the land as a result of a land dispute between the Fievie Traditional Area and a family from the Mafi Traditional Area in the Central Tongu District. The Global Agro-Development Company (GADCO), whose operations will be analysed in this book, came to the South Tongu District in 2011 and leased large tracts of land to cultivate rice in the Fievie Traditional Area.

GADCO was founded in 2009. The company was made up of a multinational team of investors and was registered in The Netherlands. The main investors were two former investment bankers from Nigeria and the UK/India respectively. The following quote from the *Financial Times* highlights their background:

> GADCO was the brainchild of Toks Abimbola, a Nigerian once based in the UK, along with Iggy Bassi, an Indian Londoner. Both were investment bankers wondering how next to pay the bills when the global financial sector went into a tailspin after Lehman

DOI: 10.4324/9781003212768-4

Brothers' 2008 collapse. Africa and rice was the answer, although neither had farming experience.

(Wallis, W., 2013, *Financial Times*, available at: https://www.ft.com/content/ee02394e-8735-11e2-bde6-00144feabdc0, last accessed: 10 October 2017)

Despite their lack of farming experience, the GADCO founders managed to attract an array of international funders. The chairperson of the company's board of directors was Lord Malloch-Brown, who was previously the Minster of State in the Foreign Office under the British Labour Party Administration of Gordon Brown and a former Chief of Staff at the United Nations.

GADCO first came to the Fievie Traditional Area in 2011, as the proximity of the Volta River and the District's climate made it a perfect location for growing rice. GADCO representatives initially approached the Paramount Chief of the Fievie Traditional Area for the acquisition of land. An agreement was negotiated whereby 1000 ha of land would be leased to GADCO for 50 years. This lease was expanded in 2013 to cover 2500 ha. Although it was impossible to receive a copy of the agreement, the company's Environmental Impact Statement (EIS) (p. 37) summarised the joint venture agreement (JVA): 1000 ha were leased to the company for 50 years, and the rent was 2.5% of the market value of rice or other cereals (or both) harvested and milled continually for the first 5 years. After 5 years, the rent would go up to 5% of the market value for the remainder of the term. Furthermore, there was a clause that GADCO had to cultivate at least 500 ha of the land within the first 12 months after signing the JVA. The EIS also mentioned the company's plans to expand the investment to 5000 ha within 3 to 4 years. According to the investors, rent was paid into a "community development fund" administered by a committee made up of chiefs and other prominent individuals. This committee was also to act as a connection between GADCO and the community.

The company initially drew upon the technical expertise of the nearby Brazil Agro Business Group for, among other things, its system of contour gravitation and cultivation techniques. It therefore entered into a management alliance with the Brazilian Agropecuária Foletto group, which provided management and technical skills as well as access to Brazilian technology (Amanor 2015, p. 14). Although GADCO initially used the Brazil Agro mill at Kpenu, it established its own mill in 2014. The company also entered into an alliance with Wienco, a company made up of Dutch and Ghanaian shareholders and one of the leading agro-input distributors in Ghana. Wienco, through its partnership with RMG Concept Ltd, which later took over GADCO, had contractual rights to distribute Syngenta seeds in Ghana. GADCO sold different types of rice and rice by-products, which were separated in the mill. Whereas the long-grain rice was sold to Finatrade (the largest food importer and distributer in Ghana, owned by a Lebanese national) and distributed across Ghana, the lower qualities were sold to the national buffer stock for school feeding programmes and to local traders. GADCO aimed to help the Ghanaian government to achieve its target of reducing Ghana's rice imports by 30% with a vision to completely meet Ghana's rice requirements by 2015 and consequently expand its operations to meet the demand of rice in the whole West African subregion (EIS 2011, p. iv). Already at the time of the first research, the company was considered the biggest commercial rice producer in West Africa.

Apart from its plantation, the company operated outgrower schemes in Ho, Hohoe, Kpong and Weta under the Copa Connect label, thus integrating over 600 smallholders into their operations. The Ho, Kpong and Weta schemes operated on government-irrigated land, and the one in Hohoe worked with smallholders on their own rainfed land. The focus of this case study, however, has been on the local "Fievie Connect" outgrower scheme, whereby the company initially worked with 45 outgrowers on parts of the land that had been acquired from the traditional authorities.

Funding and corporate social responsibility

According to one of the founders of GADCO, the company started off with an investment of USD $15 million, large parts of which were provided by the U.S. hedge fund Summit Capital, delivering 40% returns (see Wallis 2013, online). Consequently, the company has attracted more than USD $10 million in funding from various sources, such as the Syngenta Foundation for Sustainable Agriculture, the Alliance for a Green Revolution in Africa (AGRA), the Agricultural Development Company (AgDevCo), Acumen Fund and the Africa Agriculture and Trade Investment Fund (AATIF)[1]. At end of the first research, the company also received USD $500,000 from the Ghana Commercial Agriculture Project (GCAP) to expand its outgrower programme (see Chapter 2).

Most of GADCO's funders claimed to give money only to companies that comply with a variety of social and environmental criteria. However, in most cases, these criteria were rather poorly developed and weak (if any) monitoring mechanisms were in place. Although, apart from GCAP (see Chapter 2), there were no specific gender-related criteria, several of the funders captured stories of female advancement and entrepreneurship on their websites, and many of their reports and films pictured smiling "empowered" women (see, for example, the film that GADCO made with the Acumen Fund, 2013[2]).

On its website, GADCO used prominent legitimating discourses, as it declared itself to be committed to "embedding the principles of sustainability into its core business strategy and operations" and promised to "configure its business policy and invest in programs for the socio-economic advancement of women, which will deliver a 'double dividend' of improved food security and greater economic growth". Internationally prominent legitimating narratives also appeared on the company's website. For example, it was stated that

> women's contribution and role within the agri-food sector has often been overlooked. In terms of contribution in Africa: Women grow 80% of the volume of food, women process 90% of the food, women market 60% of the food, women store and transport 80% of the food. However: Women own < 1% of the land because of gender barriers and weak tenure systems, women receive < 10% of the credit received by male smallholders (due to lack of land collateral and cultural bias).

The outgrower scheme then was mentioned as the solution to some of these problems: "Improved agricultural practices, easy to adopt technologies, and access to information will enable women to produce more food and optimize hours 'in the field' under the GADCO Smallholder Program. Increased production will enhance household purchasing power and food supply". Furthermore, it was argued that "investments in education and health are vitally important in the context of women's roles in rural communities as caregivers, entrepreneurs, producers, and resource managers – all essential for economic development and food security enhancement" (GADCO website, as of 18 June 2015).

For its community–private partnership as well as its outgrower programme, GADCO has also received a great deal of positive media attention inside and outside Ghana (i.e. Darko Osei 2012; Wan 2013; Berroth 2014; Wan 2014).

Farming practices

The company continually expanded its plantation from an initial 250 ha, which were located in the southernmost tip of the floodplains of the

Adordzi and Gede creeks, to 800 ha at the time of the first research in 2014 and to 1050 ha at the time of the second research in 2016. Although initially large parts of the lower river basin were cleared, once the company started its production, the investors realised that the clayey soil was not suitable for mechanised agriculture, as their machines often got stuck. As a result, they moved upwards (see Map 4.1).

In order to irrigate the rice fields, one major canal was dug following the former current of the Gede creek to the Volta River (about 7 km in length). Two pumping stations were built on the land, as were 10 smaller irrigation/drainage canals. According to Schuppli (2016, p. 74), the company also changed the course of the Adordzi creek and dredged and deepened it to increase velocity and prevent flooding of the company's fields. The dredged creek and 10 smaller drainage/irrigation canals were

The GADCO rice farm in 2015

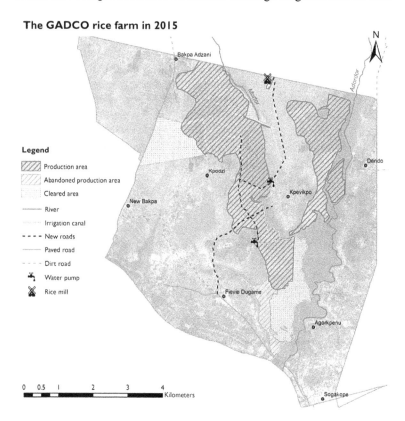

Map 4.1 The Global Agro-Development Company (GADCO) rice farm in 2015.
Source: Schuppli 2016, p. 74

used to drain excess water from the farm out into the Volta River (EIS, p. iv). In addition, contours surrounded almost the entire GADCO plantation to prevent external water infiltration into the rice farm. No fallow periods were scheduled on the fields and the company relied heavily on fertilizer use (urea and nitrogen-phosphorus-potassium) in order to continue the monocropping of rice on their plantation. A weedicide (Propanil) was sprayed aerially, significantly affecting some of the communities near the plantation, as will be highlighted in Chapter 5. Planting started at different intervals on each field, allowing for two harvests per year. The main harvesting period was from May to July (coinciding with the main rainy season, which turned out to make harvesting very difficult).

Bankruptcy of GADCO and takeover by RMG Ltd

Shortly after completion of the first field research in July 2014, GADCO went bankrupt[3]. In July 2015, the company was bought by the Swiss company RMG Concept, which re-started the farm's operations in early 2016. RMG Concept was involved in crop protection in West and Central Africa and at the time of research held exclusive rights to develop, formulate and distribute Syngenta products in Ghana and 15 other countries in West and Central Africa. The company operated in partnership with Wienco, the leading supplier of agro-inputs in Ghana, which had previously provided GADCO with pesticides. RMG Concept continued to use the name GADCO in all transactions.

The main changes resulting from the takeover concerned actual farming practices. The new company eradicated the contours introduced by GADCO and levelled the fields. It also stopped the aerial spraying of pesticides and instead used a boom sprayer mounted on a small tractor. At the time of the second research period in 2016, the company was using 1000 ha with two harvests a year, but according to the new manager, they were planning to cultivate the total 2500 ha covered in the lease document (E23, GADCO manager, Sogakope, 6 July 2016).

Although some employees were discharged as a result of the takeover (including most of the Brazilians), 15 outgrowers were added with the help of funding by the GCAP, which actually foresaw the integration of an additional 120 outgrowers (as will be discussed in Chapter 5). Some of the conditions for the outgrowers were also changed. As initially the whole group was operating together on 45 ha and dividing the profits, now each individual held a plot of 1 ha for which he or she alone was responsible.

Negotiations in a plural legal setting: the strong role of chiefs

As has been highlighted above, the land acquisition initially was negotiated with the Paramount Chief of the Fievie Traditional Area. The
investment, however, soon came to a standstill, as divisions arose
within the Fievie Traditional Area. The Paramount Stoolfather felt left
out of the agreement and managed to halt the investment by abduct-
ing one of the company's operators and involving the District Chief
Executive (DCE), who had not been informed about the investment.

> When they first came, they came to see the Paramount Chief and
> some chiefs from Agorkpo and Sogakope. So, someone informed
> me that this company had come (…). They said that they had dele-
> gated someone to come and see me and I told them that this is not
> the proceeding, because I have to be at the forefront. So, they said
> they would come to me, but because I did not assert myself, we
> held a meeting on Sunday and on Monday I heard that GADCO
> has entered the land. So, I delegated the youth to go and stop
> the project. (…) So, on a Wednesday we all agreed that Friday we
> meet in the community. But Thursday they defied my orders and
> went to the field again. So that day my boys went to hijack them.
> They took them to the community to report to the police. Because
> the DCE was also not aware, the police honor was also not aware
> of the coming of GADCO. So, it was then that they knew that we
> were serious. So, they called me, and I told them: What did I tell
> you? So, the police honorable elected me and I told him all that
> transpired and then that Saturday we all came in the community.
> GADCO also came and we started renegotiating the agreement.
>
> (E14a, Paramount Stoolfather, Sogakope, 24 May 2014)

With the Paramount Stoolfather as GADCO's new main partner, the
initial 2.5% agreement was now officially signed in the presence of the
DCE, several members of the District Assembly, and the Traditional
Council. However, no chiefs or representatives of Bakpa were present,
even though parts of Bakpa-used farmland were included in the land
deal. Similarly, the family heads whose lands were included in the deal
were not part of the negotiations. Furthermore, most of my interview
respondents were unaware of the exact terms of the contract.

   Owing to the reshuffling that had occurred, the Paramount Chief
was now in the background and the position of the Paramount
Stoolfather was considerably strengthened. As a result, a deep rift
appeared in the structure of the Fievie State and several subchiefs

questioned the legitimacy of the Paramount Chief, as his clan was not supposed to occupy this position (see Chapter 3). This tension led GADCO to pay for a large homecoming ceremony, in which the unity of the Fievie Traditional Area was celebrated with speeches, dances, music and excursions. The week-long ceremonies combined manifold references to the ancestry and tradition with notions of development and modernity in order to highlight the benefits of the investment to the community. During the main ceremony, chiefs were dressed in beautiful traditional clothes and gold chains and were carried on palanquins through the cheering and dancing crowds.

The division between the Paramount Chief and the Paramount Stoolfather seemed to have been smoothed over as a result of these celebrations, as the Stoolfather acknowledged.

There was a rift in the community, but through my instrumentality we have managed to overcome that rift. And it is GADCO, who helped to bond us together. The Paramount Chief knows that he will benefit if he is to work with me. Because I have the right to give out the land without his consent, but he cannot do it without my consent. So, he saw the reason of collaborating with me, so that he can also enjoy whatever benefit is coming.

(E14a, Paramount Stoolfather, Sogakope, 24 May 2014)

Both the GADCO manager and the Stoolfather spoke of each other as business partners. According to the manager, the 2.5% deal meant that the customary authorities, as business partners, would make sure to protect the investment (Research Diary 1, 5 May 2014). All "community issues", such as organising community consultation meetings, choosing outgrowers, and dealing with compensation claims and resistance, were left to the customary authorities to deal with, and one effect of this was a very skewed distribution of compensation payments and outgrower positions (as will be discussed in Chapter 5).

Community consultations

After the Stoolfather took over, a community meeting was called, and everyone present reportedly agreed to lease out a piece of swampy land in the river basin to the rice company. The family head, who officially owned the land, was informed of the decision but because of his advanced age could not attend the meeting. According to the old man, there was nothing he could do, even if he disagreed, since the land had been under communal use (for cattle rearing) for many years.

However, he was unhappy about the way the chiefs had gone about it and about the lack of compensation for him and his family and the destruction of shrines on the land (see Chapter 5).

Although many people remembered being told that the company would bring a "development" project to the region, several women also recollected that the project was supposed to be for them, as the quote below illustrates:

> They said it's because of us the women that they brought the project.
> (E18, female outgrower representative, Fievie-Dugame,
> 1 May 2016)

As the company realised that it was difficult to grow and harvest rice in the swampy floodplains, it left the initial area (see Map 4.1). Continual expansions saw the company move upward towards Kpodzi and Kpevikpo as well as Bakpa Adzani. In the process, vast tracts of communal land and farmland were enclosed. Although most interviewees mentioned that they initially agreed for the company to take over part of the difficult-to-cultivate and swampy floodplains near the river, no consultations were held to inform anyone about these expansions. Neither the family heads nor the Bakpa people were ever informed or consulted about the takeover of their farmland. The lack of consultation and information, as well as the lacking or inadequate compensation, led to widespread resistance (see Chapter 5).

> Initially, we were told they would take the waterlogged area but our place here, we were not informed. The people just came and we saw their truck working then we confronted them. We only went to ask them what they were doing and they told us they were bringing a development project.
> (HH:O6, male outgrower, Kpodzi, 20 June 2014)

At the time of the first research in 2014, the community was discussing a further expansion of GADCO by 120 ha in order to integrate an additional 120 outgrowers (with the help of GCAP funding). Many community meetings were held to discuss this expansion. Formally, the meetings had an aura of democracy, and women and men could freely voice their concerns and common solutions were found. Chiefs used these meetings to legitimise their actions in front of the community, praising the greater common good and the potential development that the expansion of the outgrower scheme would bring. However, it soon became clear that all decisions had been taken beforehand and the land had been given away.

The community development fund

The "community–private partnership" has received a great deal of positive media attention:

> Unlike a lease for a set fee, this arrangement tied the fortunes of community and company together; greater profits for the farm would mean greater profits for the Fievie. All costs and expenditures were to be made publicly available, and the money paid to the community would be deposited into a special account to be used exclusively on local development projects.
>
> (Wan, *The Guardian*, 22 November 2013)

Initial expert interviews with several chiefs and clan heads conveyed the impression that the "community development fund" was used for various community development purposes and that it was transparently managed.

> We use part of that money (…) for electrification of the school building and then we decided that we will use some of the money to give scholarship to brilliant but needy students. (…) It is audited anyway because anything that we do, there must be audit people to audit and see really this is the amount you've gotten for this period, how did you use it, how much is left? That transparency must be there for people to know so that (…) people will not begin to say Togbui [chief] has used our money to put up his building. The community is informed at our general meeting about the audit report.
>
> (E2, Clan Head, Fievie-Dugame, 10 April 2014)

According to the above-cited clan head, the account was managed by a committee which was made up of chiefs and elders. The chairperson of the committee was an influential local woman (a previous assembly member), and the treasurer was a local Queen Mother who came from the same clan as the Paramount Stoolfather and was also part of the Land Management Committee established by the CLS. Although Yeboah and Bugri (2016, p. 2), in their study of GADCO, argue that "getting women into such decision-making position is important in amplifying their voice, especially on issues relating to equitable use of benefits which are accruing from common resources", it is important to note that one of the main complaints of all interviewees was the lack of transparency and accountability regarding the use of the fund. Apart from a few subchiefs and relatives of the chiefs, none of the respondents was aware that the use of the GADCO fund had ever been made public. Whereas some interviewees were aware of the refurbishment of the school, the majority did not know what the money had been used for. The Paramount Queen Mother did not even know who was a member of this committee and complained that accounts had never been published (informal conversation, Research Diary 2, 6 July 2016). Having women in important positions like the Land Management Committee clearly did not automatically lead to more transparency and voice for women in general, as the following quotes, which are representative of numerous other women, illustrate.

> Many people are not happy because not many people have benefitted from the farm and the revenue being generated too is not benefitting anybody in the town. So many people are not happy for that fact.
>
> (E18, female outgrower representative, Fievie-Dugame,
> 1 May 2016)

> I don't know what they are using the money for, because up till now we don't even have good drinking water in the town.
>
> (HH:LL6, young woman, Kpodzi, 20 May 2014)

During the community meetings, various people confronted the chiefs about the use of money and were always told to wait until another time. During the first field research, several dates where the chiefs were supposed to account for the use of funds were set, but the appointments were postponed again and again. During the second field research, still no accounts had been made, causing a lot of anger and disillusion with the chiefs in the communities.

Although it was clear that only a very limited portion of the GADCO rent had been spent on community development purposes, the Paramount Stoolfather mentioned that the fund was channelled towards the various land litigation cases that the traditional area was involved in.

> GADCO is actually having a tremendous impact on that. Every month we take 2.5% from them and that is a lot – on the average it is about 15,000 GHC a month (USD 4700). When it reaches 5%, that will amount to 30,000 and that depends on the size. If they increase, we will even be taking 40,000 GHC a month. It is a lot of money. We appreciate it. I am telling you, we appreciate it a lot. As a result now, you can't toy with us, because we can match you, we have the resources. They are actually helping us a lot, they are helping us. (…) The money is used for community development. And litigation is very expensive. People are litigating us over the

land, and without resources you can't litigate. So with the help of GADCO, we are able to pay our legal fees without any challenge.

(E14a, Paramount Stoolfather, Sogakope, 24 May 2014)

Despite these obvious shortcomings of the "community development fund", the company officially adhered to its socially sustainable business model. However, when questioned, the company's managers mentioned that they did not care what the money was used for.

What they use the money for is none of our business. If you do business with me, it is not up to you to tell me to share the money with my wife. We have our business structures and they have their own. We don't meddle with their way of doing things.

(E23, GADCO manager, Sogakope, 6 July 2016)

Position of the government

Owing to their various "socially minded" funders, GADCO had to comply with relevant government regulations. So they involved both the Lands Commission and the Environmental Protection Agency (EPA).

We have a consultant and he made us aware of this, but no other farm, not even the government farm over there does it – they don't even have an EPA permit. Because of our investors, we just try to be very socially responsible or honest people.

(E14, former GADCO manager, Vume, 22 June 2014)

When the company first arrived, they had hired a surveyor to make a map of the area, which was taken to the Lands Commission to check whether there were any disputes registered on the land. The only dispute found related to Bakpa land that previously had been given out to Galten Ltd and had now been included in the contract with GADCO. Since there was still an injunction on the land, GADCO was not yet using the land but rather waiting for the court case to be resolved in favour of Fievie (E14, former GADCO manager, 22 June 2014). An Environmental Impact Assessment (EIA) was carried out in 2011, and the company was also supposed to pay water taxes, which, however, they were resisting with the help of the traditional authorities.

We are currently charged for a water extraction permit from the Water Resources Commission and Fievie chiefs don't want to pay that anymore. They are telling us not to pay and they will take it up. But yes, we get charged for pumping water from this river. (…) I don't know the details of it, but the Water Resources Commission is in Accra. I actually think it is ridiculous, look at this river, it empties into the ocean, and you are charging people who are making food, it's ridiculous.

(E14, former GADCO manager, 22 June 2014)

RMG Ltd revised its Environmental Management Plan (EMP) in 2015. Although both the EIS (2011) and the EMP (2016) are fairly comprehensive documents, outlining various social and environmental risks posed by the company's operations and identifying distinct mitigation measures for these risks, many of the measures announced were implemented only partially if at all. Even though GADCO involved all of the relevant regional ministries, several District Government Officials mentioned a general dissatisfaction with the way that GADCO bypassed them and negotiated directly with the customary authorities, who were also the main beneficiaries of these deals. According to the former DCE, there was a great deal of secrecy on the part of customary authorities when it came to the GADCO land acquisition and the government was only ever involved in case of problems.

It is a partnership between them and the Fievie people, so they are handling it. It is only when there is conflict or they feel cheated that they will run to us. But once they are sure they are doing their own thing and District Assembly is not worrying them, they are fine.

(E5a, DCE, Sogakope, 22 April 2014)

The DCE also decided to impose a rice tax on GADCO in order to generate some funds for the district. Again, GADCO in collaboration with the Fievie authorities resisted it.

Our relationship with the government is a bit difficult. We have the local government here, the DCE, and they now want to tax every bag of rice. That's actually why the chiefs came, to ask them why? We had a meeting with the DCE and we are just thinking of how to work this out. It is not a tax on GADCO, it is a tax on the people we supply. So, they will have to pay something like 50 pesewas[4] more per bag that crosses the bridge. Again, to show our community relationship, we called up Zikpuitor [Stoolfather], told him about it, and he said he would come.

(E14, former GADCO manager, 22 June 2014)

It appeared that the hands of the DCE and other local government officials were often tied because of their need to adhere to central government policy, which heavily promoted commercial agriculture, but possibly also because of close connections between local chiefs and the national government elite. Although state authorities had not been involved in the land deal, the district needed to forward production data of GADCO to the central government in order to show that they had created an enabling environment for the company.

The requirement to render account of having created an enabling business environment, as well as the positive media coverage that GADCO received and the public support that various government officials had voiced for the company[5] made it difficult for local government officials to raise opposition.

> The government is not involved, not at all. But now the government is happy with GADCO. They are even claiming the project as theirs. It has become the flagship of the government. The government is now taking the credit (laughing), but let them take the credit, it's theirs.
>
> (E14a, Paramount Stoolfather, Sogakope, 24 May 2014)

This also explains why – even though various governmental agencies were aware of the adverse effects of the GADCO investment, as outlined in the next chapter – little was done to address the complaints.

Notes

1 While *Acumen Fund* relies on funding from the Rockefeller foundation, as well as individual philanthropists, some of GADCO's other funders receive money directly from international development actors, such as the Department for International Development (i.e. AgDevCo) or the Gates Foundation (i.e. AGRA).

2 Interestingly, the protagonist in the GADCO film was a lady we met several times during the research: the sister of one of the chiefs – a rather powerful and wealthy lady – who, in the film claimed to be a poor widow benefitting from the GADCO investment.

3 The reasons for the bankruptcy are unknown. While local people believe that mismanagement (i.e. the very high wages paid to management staff) and lack of farming knowledge were the cause, an interview with the former GADCO manager indicated that major harvest loss in 2014 dealt a blow to the company's finances.

4 50 pese was equal about 15 US pennies (based on the oanda.com exchange rate of 22 June 2014).

5 At the GADCO mill opening ceremony on 9 April 2014, various government officials, including the Vice President of Ghana, pledged their support to GADCO and highlighted the company as a best-practice example of foreign investment.

References

Amanor, K.S. (2015). *Rising powers and rice in Ghana: China, Brazil and African agricultural development*. Future Agricultures Working Paper 123. Brighton, UK: University of Sussex.

Berroth, K. (2014). 'Impact begins inside the company'. *Huffington Post*. Available at: https://www.huffingtonpost.com/acumen/impact-begins-inside-the-_b_5288120.html. Last accessed: 14 February 2018.

Darko Osei, R. (2012). '*GADCO- A holistic approach to tackling low agricultural incomes. UNDP Case Study*'. New York: United Nations Development Programme (UNDP).

Schuppli, D. (2016). *The impact of large-scale land acquisitions on land use and local actor's access to land*. MA thesis, Berne, Switzerland: University of Berne.

Wallis, W. (2013). 'Ghana rice venture points new way ahead'. *Financial Times*. Available at: https://www.ft.com/content/ee02394e-8735-11e2-bde6-00144feabdc0. Last accessed: 10 October 2017.

Wan, J. (2013). 'Ghanaian rice growers cultivate a food security solution'. *The Guardian*. Available at: https://www.theguardian.com/global-development-professionals-network/2013/nov/22/ghanaian-rice-growers-cultivate-food-security-solution. Last accessed: 25 April 2018.

Wan, J. (2014). 'Freundliche Übernahme. Reisanbau in Ghana'. Welt-Sichten – Magazin für globale Entwicklung und ökumenische Zusammenarbeit. Available at: https://www.weltsichten.org/artikel/20924/ghana-freundliche-uebernahme. Last accessed: 25 April 2018.

Yeboah, E. and J. Bugri (2016). 'Building innovative partnership to bridge gender gaps in large scale land investments, insights from the GADCO – Fievie model in Ghana'. Paper presented at the *Annual World Bank Conference on Land and Poverty*, Washington, DC (14–18 March 2016).

5 "They said they were bringing a development project" – the evolution of local livelihoods and impacts of the large-scale land investment

The historical evolution of local livelihoods: building of the Akosombo Dam

Being riparian communities, people in the South Tongu District used to depend on the Volta River for their livelihoods. Since the earliest settlement period, many communities in the area were reliant on river and creek fishing as well as on farming. An abundance of fish swarmed the Volta River and its various tributaries, and the annual overflows of the river made the soil very fertile for seasonal farming activities (Nyendu 2006, pp. 7–8). According to Tsikata (2012, p. 85), the inhabitants of the Lower Volta "had developed a successful system of livelihoods organized around the seasonal flooding of the Volta".

When the floods receded in December, women started to engage in clam picking – an activity that lasted about 6 months, during a time when many men seasonally migrated upstream to engage in fishing in the Volta River (Tsikata 2012, p. 101). Clam picking was "the most valuable activity in the fishing industry" (Moxon 1984, p. 190) and "the economic mainstay of downstream riverine communities" (Barnes 1964, p. 2). Several communities thus were said to have been prosperous in the past, mainly as a result of the booming clam industry.

Their fortunes, however, changed with the building of the Akosombo Hydroelectric Power Dam in the late 1960s and the construction of the Kpong Dam in 1982. Although the dam was seen "as a technological triumph and a symbol of modern nationhood" by most Ghanaians (Tsikata 2012, p. 1), its construction had severe socioeconomic consequences for the downstream villages, including most communities in the South Tongu District. As a result of the need to keep enough water upstream to run the turbines of the dam, the regular flow of the Volta River was impeded, which not only prevented fish from flowing downstream but also led to the growth of

DOI: 10.4324/9781003212768-5

various weeds and water hyacinth, making fishing very difficult. The weeds also caused the region manifold health problems, including increased incidences of schistosomiasis (bilharzia) and malaria (Nyendu 2006, p. 9). Owing to the unnaturally slow flow of the river, clams were now buried deep in the sand and mud, making them unreachable for the female clam-pickers. Both the clam and fishing industries went into decline, throwing many households into poverty and leading to large out-migration. Numerous fishermen went upstream north of Akosombo to engage in fishing, and others migrated to the cities to find jobs (ibid., p. 9). The clam-picking past of Fievie-Dugame is still very visible today, as one can find countless shells on the ground in certain areas of the village.

The building of the Akosombo Dam has also affected the four study communities, albeit to different extents. Bakpa Adzani is the most affected of the four, as it was previously located in the North Tongu District and, as a result of the construction of the Akosombo Dam, was completely flooded in 1963. Together with another Bakpa community, the village was resettled to the South Tongu District. Whereas various people decided to migrate north to continue with their fishing activities, others had to adapt to their new circumstances and focus their livelihoods on farming and, in the case of women, trading.

As was highlighted in Chapter 3, Kpodzi and Kpevikpo were established over a century ago for the purposes of cattle rearing and hence were somewhat less dependent on the natural course of the Volta River for their livelihoods. However, the villagers also used the various fishponds in the floodplains, which, whenever the river overflooded its banks, would fill up with fish and support the whole community.

> We just used nets which we cast into the flooded river. Before the Akosombo Dam was constructed, flooding came from the Volta River to the whole area, where the rice farm is now. So, we only went into the floods by foot, and sometimes in our dug-out canoes to cast our nets to harvest or catch fish. But when the Dam was constructed, the flooding did not come anymore. Since the floods stopped, it was rainfall that flooded the place for us to catch fish.
>
> (B15, middle-aged woman, Kpevikpo, 1 May 2016)

In general, various interviewees mentioned that the construction of the Akosombo Dam had a huge impact on their livelihoods, which became much less diverse and increasingly dependent on rainfall for their farming activities and for the flooding of the fishponds.

We, the people of Tongu, were fishermen and when the dam was constructed, it blocked the river and weed took over so we didn't get fish again. We, the Ewe people, got money from clams to build our houses, look after our children in school and everything, but now the Akosombo made weed come on the water and we didn't get fish to catch and no clam to extract as well (…). Though the dam is good, because it provides us with electricity, what we lost is greater than the electricity we got. (…) (…) If it were not the illegal mining [galamsey] that came to exist, Tongu towns would be extinct because that is the work that the youths have resorted to. For the Akosombo Dam, it only came to destroy Tongu.

(E10b, Paramount Queen Mother, Fievie-Dugame, 1 May 2016)

This quote already indicates that illegal mining has become an important source of income for the study communities, which in recent years have additionally been affected by climatic changes and frequent droughts that have made farming more unreliable, thus putting increasing strains on the once-prosperous communities.

Livelihoods and gender relations in the study area before the arrival of GADCO

According to the 2010 Ghana Population and Housing Census (Ghana Statistical Service 2014), the South Tongu District had an estimated population of 87,950 people (45.5% were male and 54.5% were female) and 87.1% of the population lived in rural areas. However, statistics for the study villages were unreliable, and numbers given by the District Statistical Officer and the respective village heads and chiefs differed vastly. Only Fievie-Dugame provided a gender breakdown, which shows a huge difference between males and females. The right-most column of Table 5.1 shows government estimates of the population.

Main livelihood activities prior to GADCO's arrival

According to the 2010 Population and Housing Census (PHC), 90.4% of the population were working in the informal sector and 6% were working in the public sector. About 56.3% of households in the district were engaged in agriculture, and the majority of them (90.2%) were engaged in crop farming. The main food crops were maize and cassava, tomatoes and okra, and the main cash crop was pepper (chili). The average agricultural land holding was about one hectare per household, and most small-scale farmers used crop rotation,

Table 5.1 Population statistics of study villages

	Total (provided by customary authority)	Male	Female	Total (provided by the government)
Fievie-Dugame	673	287	386	408
Kpodzi	220	Not provided	Not provided	30
Kpevikpo	185	Not provided	Not provided	105
Bakpa Adzani	315	Not provided	Not provided	Not provided

inter-cropping and mixed farming practices. The PHC also recorded a total of 6496 livestock keepers owning a combined 116,106 animals (Ghana Statistical Services 2014).

This broader district data was reflected in the study villages, where almost everybody was working in the informal sector and the main livelihood activities were farming, trading, the sale of fuelwood and charcoal, and the operation of motorbike taxis (okada). Even though climatic changes and increasing droughts clearly were making farming more risky, older men and women were still engaged in agriculture. Many young men, however, were not interested in agriculture anymore and were temporarily migrating to engage in illegal gold mining (galamsey) in other areas of Ghana and in Cote d'Ivoire. According to some informants, several men had died in the mines. A significant number of (mostly older and wealthy) men were also engaged in cattle rearing, specifically in the study villages of Kpodzi and Kpevikpo.

Women generally were engaged in diverse income-earning activities: whereas most women were farmers (often farming their own small plots and helping on their husband's parcels), many also worked in food processing, trading and selling food, and several younger women had also migrated to nearby towns and cities to find employment. The collection and sale of firewood provided numerous poor and landless women with an income, and some wealthier women in the study communities ran small businesses, namely shops or chop bars (small restaurants).

Given the limited availability of paid employment, most livelihoods continued to be closely linked to the land and the manifold natural resources found on the land, as will be highlighted below.

Land use and its relation to livelihoods

Schuppli's (2016) study on Land Use and Land Cover Change (LULCC) documents that, prior to the arrival of GADCO, the area was dominated by grassland, which covered about 54% of the study area in 2009 and was used mainly for grazing cattle. Within the Fievie Traditional Area, there were about 100 cattle owners, most of them owning between 50 and 300 cows. However, many of them also looked after other people's livestock, which made some herd sizes exceed 1000 cows. During the dry season, cattle were moved to the floodplains, where the greater soil moisture allowed grasses to sprout, when there was no more fodder available on the general grazing areas. Cattle owners, most of whom were male, were organised through a cattle owner association at the district as well as at the regional level. The cattle owners also engaged in farming and held smaller domestic animals for their daily income, and cattle were instead held as a form of wealth.

Apart from pasture, the vast areas of communally used lands held a number of important common pool resources and were also used for seasonal agriculture (see Map 5.1).

Thatch for roofing and reeds used for weaving mats were collected in the floodplains. The bush and woodlands as well as forests and the many scattered trees and bushes on grasslands also served as the main source

Productive services of jointly used areas in 2009

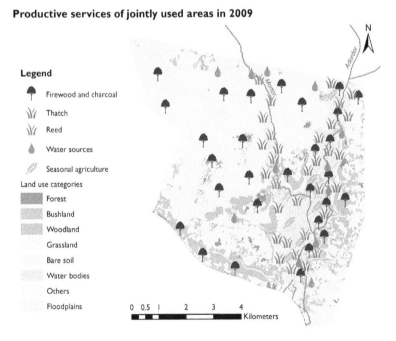

Map 5.1 Productive uses of the commons.

Source: Schuppli 2016, p. 116

of firewood to local communities. Furthermore, the collection and sale of fuelwood (and, in some cases, charcoal made from tree stumps) constituted a major income-generating activity for many women and were also seen as "buffer" activities in times of distress (i.e. when quick money was needed to pay for hospital bills, buy food or provide for other emergencies), thus playing an important role for households' resilience.

> Sometimes when the harvest season doesn't come, it becomes very difficult for some few days but we usually manage to get some food and wait for the season. (…) Sometimes we have to go to the bush and cut down some trees to make charcoal to sell and get some money for food.
>
> (B3, elderly man, Bakpa Adzani, 18 June 2016)

In addition, Neem trees were used by local women for various medicinal purposes, and in the two Bakpa villages, women also used the fruits from the Baobab tree to make a local porridge, which was sold by the roadside. Other wild fruits, such as wild mangoes, could be collected on the communally used land.

The two creeks as well as various water ponds and small dams also provided drinking water to all four communities. Whereas most of the ponds dried up during the dry season, the largest ones contained water the whole year round and were of crucial importance to pastoralists for the watering of cattle (Schuppli 2016, p. 69). The numerous man-made fishponds in the floodplains also provided important resources to local livelihoods. Even though the ponds were owned by individual families, fish could be caught by anybody living in the area when the creeks overflooded their banks. The use reverted to the owners during the dry season. In the rainy season, people used hooks to catch fish all over the floodplains. Prior to the flood, the pond owners put some branches into the water to create a spawning ground for fish. After the flood receded, fish grew and multiplied in the ponds. As soon as the water was drying out, fish were harvested by the owners and their helpers with the use of nets and buckets.

Most of the fish were dried and smoked after harvest and then kept for home consumption. Sometimes, surplus fish were also sold to derive an income. Whereas during the rainy season both men and women were collecting fish, in the dry season, as the use reverted to the family, it was mainly men who engaged in this practice. Women were generally the ones to sell leftover fish on the market. The importance of fish to local diets cannot be overstated, as people ate fish with every single meal, and it was often mentioned that they would rather not eat than eat a meal without fish.

Fish is important for us, because without fish we cannot eat.

(Household Interview, fishpond owner, Fievie-Dugame, 3 March
2015, *DS)

Farming and trading

Even though, according to Schuppli's study on LULCC, farmland
covered only 20.8% of the study area in 2009, the majority of the population in the four study communities was engaged in rainfed small-
scale agriculture, growing traditional subsistence crops, such as maize
and cassava. Most households also produced cash crops, mainly pepper and groundnuts, and some wealthier families operated medium-
scale mango, cashew and woodlot plantations. Most farm plots were
located near the settlements and depended solely on rainfall for irrigation. People living near the floodplains, especially in Kpevikpo, also
used the seasonally flooded areas for agriculture during the dry season, as the greater soil moisture in these areas enabled farmers to cultivate crops with higher water requirements, such as okra and tomatoes.
In all four study villages, both women and men cultivated cash crops
and subsistence crops. However, owing to gendered roles and responsibilities, the size of their farms differed.

Although pesticides (both chemical and organic) were used by a
majority of farmers, the use of fertilizers was low because of the floodplains' high soil fertility, which was maintained by annual crop rotation and consequent fallow periods. There were two rainy seasons in
the area, but many respondents reported that rainfall patterns had
become unpredictable, leading to major crop and harvest losses.

Only a few wealthy households had access to tractors to plough
their fields, and others were either hiring tractors or using hoes to
manually prepare the ground. Ploughing was generally done by men;
this provided an obstacle to female heads-of-household, who had to
hire labour or ask male relatives for help. Many young men also
worked as day labourers on richer people's fields, as these relied on
hired labour for their crop production and harvest.

Cash crops were either sold on the local market in Sogakope or
Dabala or sold to traders. Pepper was generally sold to traders, coming
from as far as Togo and Benin. Trading and selling crops as well as
processed foods (such as Gari, cassava dough or small pastries) in the
market or directly in the communities were done exclusively by women.

Although cattle rearing was practiced mainly by better-off families,
most households kept some small livestock (guinea fowls, turkeys,
pigs, goats and chicken). Cattle rearing, which was seen as a

prestigious activity, was done only by men, but women usually were in charge of looking after the smaller animals. These were kept mainly as assets to be sold in case of major distress, such as illness or drought.

In all study communities, people reported to depend more on their own production for food security rather than on the market (even though all villagers bought some food on the market). The main staple crops (corn and cassava) were used to produce local meals such as Banku and Akple.

Gendered division of labour

Polygamy was still widespread in the study area; most often, men lived with one of their wives while their other wife or wives were heading separate households. Even though men were supposed to look after all of their wives equally, many women in polygamous households claimed to receive no monetary benefits from their husbands and thus were in charge of feeding their own families, living as de facto female heads-of-household.

Marriage patterns, however, were changing in the Fievie Traditional Area. Most of the older female research participants had been married off at a very young age, sometimes betrothed to an older relative. In contrast, most younger women mentioned that nowadays they chose their partners and there were increasing numbers of people living in monogamous or informal marriages. Informal marriages were particularly common among young people, among whom it was assumed that once you got pregnant from a man, you were married. There was, however, a high break-up rate among these young, informally married couples, and many young girls ended up going back to their mothers or grandmothers, who then took care of their (great) grandchildren.

The high number of young single mothers added to the already-large numbers of female heads-of-household, which included widows as well as women from polygamous marriages who did not live with their husbands. In some cases, these households consisted only of grandmothers and children; in others, young mothers also lived with their mothers and children or with other relatives. In most households (including in those where men and women lived together), all adults appeared to contribute somehow to the household economy.

Contributions made to the household economy clearly differed according to locally entrenched gender roles and responsibilities. Although both women and men in the study communities engaged in farming subsistence and cash crops, men often depended crucially on the labour of their wives and children. In addition to farming, women were mostly in charge of selling crops on the market or to traders, and many women also engaged in small-scale trading activities. Very few women, mostly from wealthy families, ran small shops or businesses in the communities. The collection and sale of firewood and charcoal, on the other hand, were done mainly by poorer women. Like trading, they were considered "feminine tasks", which could not be undertaken by men for fear of ridicule.

A factor that united all women was that they were mainly in charge of all reproductive activities, such as looking after their children (and, in many cases, grandchildren), cooking, cleaning, fetching water and firewood, and taking care of sick and elderly family members. The fact that most women engaged in both productive and reproductive activities meant that they generally had much longer work days than men and consequently more time constraints.

Whereas some respondents from monogamous households also reported increasing engagement by men who helped with fetching water, cooking, or looking after the children, women generally complained about men's irresponsibility and their lack of support to the household economy. Many women, regardless of marriage status, thus mentioned being the main person in charge of looking after their families.

> My other brothers are all living out of town so I'm responsible to see to it that there is food available for everyone. I do that by collecting firewood and sometimes I do that with my children. When there is no money and no food in the house, the children wouldn't go to school. They would go with me to the bush to collect firewood before I'll get some money to buy food for them.
> (B5, elderly widow, Bakpa Adzani, 18 June 2016)

Perceptions and livelihood impacts of the GADCO land acquisition

By looking at the location of the GADCO investment, one can already see power dynamics at play, as most of the land enclosed by the company was originally used by settler communities. However, not only were the losses distributed unevenly, but also compensation payments, employment and integration into the company's local outgrower scheme were skewed, and elites and relatives of chiefs were much more likely to be compensated and hired as outgrowers. It will be highlighted that although women were supposed to be the main beneficiaries of the investment, mainly wealthy women benefited from the outgrower scheme and that the company's general employment rather reinforced the devaluation of women's labour. Furthermore, women were most affected by the loss of common pool resources.

Distribution of losses

According to Schuppli's study on LULCC in the affected communities, in 2015 GADCO had enclosed approximately 931 ha of communally used land and 92 ha of farmland, the latter located mainly near Bakpa Adzani and in the uplands around Kpodzi. Together with Galten Ltd. – the abandoned Jatropha plantation near Bakpa Adzani – about 1300 ha of land had been enclosed by large-scale investors (see Map 5.2).

The map shows that Kpevikpo has been completely enclosed by the plantation, and even though a dirt road connecting Kpevikpo to Fievie-Dugame had been built, the village had been cut off through the company's irrigation canal. Also evident is the fact that Bakpa Adzani was squeezed in between the expanding operations of GADCO on the right

Land Use / Land Cover Map 2015

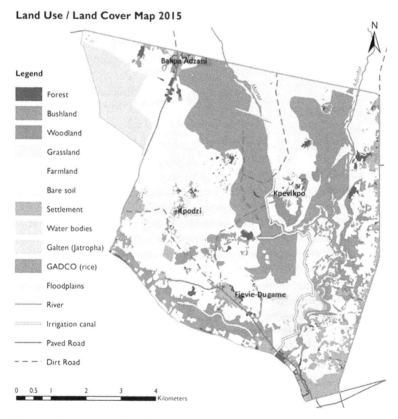

Map 5.2 Land use and land cover in 2015.

Source: Schuppli 2016, p. 74

and Galten Ltd. on the left. Even though Galten had already left the area at the time of the research, the village community was not allowed to use the land until the ongoing court case was resolved.

Loss of common pool resources (pasture, water and trees)

As demonstrated by Schuppli (2016), the vast majority of land acquired by GADCO was previously used communally. In the process of transforming the commons into a rice plantation, more and more grazing land was made inaccessible to cattle rearers. In particular, the swampy areas in the floodplains, which were used for dry-season grazing, were largely enclosed by the plantation. Furthermore, movement between different grazing fields was curtailed by the rice farm and the various irrigation canals. Coupled with the destruction of water ponds used for watering cattle, these changes provided a threat to cattle rearers' livelihoods.

Furthermore, the company destroyed many ponds, creeks and dams used for drinking water, and some of the few remaining ponds were poisoned by pesticides. The company had cut off Kpodzi and Kpevikpo from their main water supply by re-directing the two rivers and destroying a major water pond that had been used for both humans and animals. Even though GADCO dug a new pond for the area, the villagers frequently mentioned that it was not well built, as it was small and the runoff from the farm made the water unusable. Bakpa Adzani was also affected by the destruction of a small dam. The retained water was previously used especially by poorer people from the community, who could not afford to buy water from the standpipe in the village. In all villages, women, who were generally in charge of collecting water for the household, were affected the most by the loss of water supplies and had to find alternative means.

The vast majority of trees used to make firewood and charcoal for sale, as well as the Baobab trees, which grew near the Bakpa communities, were uprooted and removed for the rice plantation. Other resources that were largely lost because of the felling of trees and destruction of other plants included thatch (used for roofing) and reeds (used for weaving baskets and mats). However, these were mentioned much less frequently by respondents – an indication that they were less important to local livelihoods than other common pool resources, such as water and fuelwood.

GADCO's Environmental Impact Statement (EIS) (p. 36) also referred to four local shrines on the land. Three of them were especially mentioned by several interviewees. Although the company's EIS guaranteed that the sacred groves would be protected during land preparation and kept open once the fields were planted, this (according to my respondents) was not the case and shrines had been destroyed.

> Before the company came, a part of the land was a sacred forest, home to three Gods. Anyevove, the main God, after which the forest was named, lived in a pond that never dried up. He had two assistant Gods, who also lived in water, but they sometimes died. The whole forest had been preserved for the Gods, so nobody was allowed to do farming there.
>
> (FGD2, differently affected men, 11 May 2014)

According to the family head, who was the owner of large parts of the communal land taken by GADCO, the three Gods – Anyevove, Kpevi and Djanego – were responsible for rainfall on the land. The family head mentioned that the chiefs had not asked him for permission to take his land and that he was too old (over 100 years) to go and pour libations and slaughter an animal to appease the Gods. As a result, there had been no rainfall on the land since the company came (Research Diary 1, 23 April 2014). Many people shared this perception of decreasing rainfall due to GADCO's operations. Whereas some villagers attributed it to the destruction of the shrines, others ascribed it to the reduced tree cover, yet others believed that GADCO had a machine that was used to disperse clouds. The lack of rainfall was a big problem, especially during the first research in 2014, as a prolonged drought had destroyed many crops, causing fears of food insecurity.

Loss of fishponds

The company also destroyed most local fishponds. The construction of the irrigation canal and of the dam along the creek Adordzi meant that even fishponds outside the company's concession area were no longer flooded. This not only was problematic from the fishpond owner's point of view but led to a general reduction in the availability of fish. Many villagers reported having to buy fish on the market as a result.

> We used to catch fish and get firewood from there. Our forefathers dug ponds in the water logs and fishes remain in them when the water dries up but all these things were destroyed and now we buy even firewood for cooking.
>
> (HH:LL1, elderly widow, Fievie-Dugame, 4 June 2014)

The reduced availability of fish hit the poorest households the hardest, as they could not afford to buy fish on the market. Eating a meal without fish was culturally inconceivable for many people. Furthermore, women who used to sell fish on the market or in the village now also lost that source of earning.

Loss of farmland

GADCO enclosed approximately 92 ha of farmland, mainly in the area of Bakpa Adzani and Kpodzi. For Bakpa Adzani, this was the second enclosure of large tracts of their farmland by a foreign investor, as in 2009 Fievie already had leased out large tracts of Bakpa-used farmland to Galten Ltd. According to Schuppli (2016), in 2015, 40.8 ha of farmland were enclosed by Galten. Although many villagers from Kpodzi were able to access new farmland, the loss of land was particularly severe for Bakpa Adzani, as little suitable farmland was left near the community.

> Their coming has taken our farmlands and also they have uprooted the trees that we survived on for charcoal when things became very tough. My two acres of cassava were cleared (…) the land there is not even sufficient for us because we are many and only have small, small lands so access to new land is not possible.
>
> (B3, elderly man, Bakpa Adzani, 18 June 2016)

Qualitative data also indicates that the amount of farmland lost to GADCO's operations was considerably larger than suggested by the numbers estimated via remote sensing, as both seasonally cultivated plots and land that had been left fallow were not visible with remote sensing (Schuppli 2016, p. 83). Various respondents from Kpevikpo deplored that several crops (such as okra, tomato and garden egg) that did well in the lowlands were not doing well in the uplands. A walk through Kpevikpo revealed the difficulties of planting certain crops, such as okra. As the rains had been delayed, one could see numerous plots of shrivelled-up okra and pepper plants. This was all the more striking when compared with the lush green, professionally irrigated plantation of GADCO, which was just a few meters away.

Both remote-sensing data from Schuppli's (2016) study on LULCC and qualitative data collected indicate that settlers were affected predominantly by the loss of farmland, which can be seen as a direct result of their lack of rights under customary land tenure, which makes it much easier for customary authorities to legitimise the appropriation of land from them. Within settler communities, both women and men and wealthy and poor people were affected by the loss of land, but gender and wealth had an effect on how well people managed to cope with the loss of land.

Effects of agrochemicals

In its 2011 EISs, GADCO outlined potential impacts of agrochemicals (urea, nitrogen-phosphorus-potassium, Propanil and Glycosate) on the environment and the communities. It was conceded that agrochemicals along with oil and grease leakages from the pumping stations potentially pollute the two perennial rivers on which various communities depended for water, bathing and washing. Interestingly, however, only five potentially affected communities were identified and the four study communities, which also depended on these streams, were not mentioned (EIS 2011, p. 32). As mitigation measures, GADCO proposed to apply herbicides only when inevitable and to use fertilizers solely at the onset of the planting season and to re-direct drained water back into the canal for irrigation (p. 40).

It was not verifiable whether GADCO implemented the measures outlined above. However, people from Kpevikpo, Kpodzi and Fievie-Dugame complained about the runoff from agrochemicals into their water ponds, which had negative health effects on both humans and cattle. Several people mentioned having to go to hospital. Unexplained deaths of cattle were also attributed to chemicals in the water.

In 2014, GADCO constructed an airstrip and started spraying weedicides aerially. This was one of the major complaints voiced by many respondents and it came up again and again at community meetings. The harmful effects of the aerial spraying of pesticides were felt predominantly by the three settler communities that were closest to the plantation. Many people reported health hazards from the spraying, as water sources were contaminated and the company even sprayed directly on people working in the fields or on children going to school.

> The spraying affects us – it falls on our community directly. My father can't walk anymore, so he usually sits outside the house. They spray him directly and all the trees around us are dying.
> (Woman from Kpodzi at community meeting, 18 May 2014)

In particular, Kpevikpo, which had been completely encircled by the rice plantation, was heavily struck by the spraying of pesticides. All interviewees from Kpevikpo complained that the aerial spraying poisoned their farms and had destroyed many people's crops. RMG, however, stopped spraying weedicides aerially when they took over the plantation.

Several interviewees were also concerned about GADCO's heavy use of fertilizers and lacking fallow periods. They feared that the soil would lose its fertility and that they would be unable to use it if the company ever left the area. The potential loss of soil fertility because of the company's operations was also acknowledged in GADCO's EIS (2011, p. 38), which mentioned that

> [l]and harrowing may expose the soil to nutrient leaching, espe-cially when the place is heavily flooded in the rainy season. In the event of flooding of the area, draining the land could lead to top soil degradation and subsequent soil fertility loss.

When RMG took over the farm in 2016, they completely levelled the land, thus removing most of the top soil layer in the process, which in the view of various concerned locals further increased the likelihood of soil degradation.

Distribution of gains

Apart from the "community development fund", which at the time of research had yielded only few benefits, the main gains arising from GADCO's operations in the local area were related to compensation pay-ments, employment creation, the local outgrower scheme, infrastructure creation and the benefits from the increased availability of rice in the area.

Compensation

GADCO's EIS (2011) did not identify the loss of farmland as a poten-tial threat to small-scale farmers. According to the former GADCO manager, compensation was paid to all people who were "legally" farming in the area. At the time of the first research, he mentioned that the company had indemnified at least 50 people and some were yet to receive reparation. Compensation payments were handled in collabora-tion with the Fievie chiefs, and only those villagers who previously had asked the chiefs for permission to farm on the land were reimbursed.

> So, anyone that was genuinely farming in an area that we were putting under cultivation, that is actually on Fievie land. A lot of them did not get permission to farm there, they just went there

and farmed. They may be from Fievie or not, but they are supposed to go and get permission.

(E4, former GADCO manager, 22 June 2014)

As has been emphasised before, most of the farmland that was destroyed by the company had previously been used by settler communities (mainly Bakpa Adzani and Kpodzi). However, it was notable that, out of the 30 households that were initially questioned about compensation for farmland, those who claimed to have received reparation came mainly from Fievie-Dugame but that only a few people from Kpodzi and Kpevikpo had been indemnified. Most of the compensated persons were chiefs or relatives of the chiefs (both women and men) as well as other locally important citizens, but the majority of interviewees mentioned not having received any reparation. Compensation amounts differed: some people claimed that everybody had received the same amount regardless of acreage lost (but mentioned different amounts) and others said that the amount depended on the crops that were lost (not the actual land that had been lost). The following excerpt from an interview with an elderly woman from Kpevikpo underlines the strong role of chiefs in handing out payments and the importance of having connections to the elite.

KL: How did they decide how much you should be compensated for?
They have decided that by themselves, the committee which is the leadership of the community here, which should stand and bargain on our behalf have not done that, because they are corrupt. They only left the issue to the farm management to decide and they have only given me 400 GHS and my husband 500 GHS[1].

KL: Some people didn't get any compensation at all. Do you know how it was decided? Some of you got something and others didn't get anything at all.
It is as a result of the corruption among the elders of this community, the committee members. There are some people who would even go and set fire to their own farms and go and report that GADCO has destroyed their farms. The committee, because they are related and have something to do with those people, they would get compensation for them. They would write the names of their children that they have also destroyed their farm, but some of us who don't have that link with them, they would even see that our farms are destroyed, but they wouldn't fight for us.

(B14, elderly widow, Kpevikpo, 24 June 2016)

People from Bakpa Adzani were compensated only after mounting heavy resistance, which led to a District Security Council Meeting being called and a consequent evaluation of individual crop loss.

> We organized a joint District Security Council meeting to try set-
> tling the dispute and we came up with a proposal and brought on
> board agricultural valuation experts to come and value the crops
> destroyed so they pay compensation. GADCO came back and said
> the compensation was a bit too high for them but we told them the
> valuation was done by an individual expert so they have to pay.
>
> (E5a, District Chief Executive [DCE], Sogakope, 22 May 2014)

A copy of the list handed to GADCO as a result of the evaluation was provided. It shows that 26 Bakpa farms, covering a total of 69.5 acres (about 30 ha), were affected by the plantation; this appears to be in line with remote sensing data collected by Schuppli (2016). However, in a letter to the District Security Council (DISEC) and the District Assemblies of North and South Tongu, GADCO claimed that nine of the affected farmers presented themselves to the company and that they claimed to be the only Bakpa people damaged by the planta-tion. The company reimbursed them for a total of 14 acres of land, handing out a total of USD $9895 in compensation payments. Most of the remunerated farmers were unwilling to speak, as the money they received had created a lot of resentment and conflict within the community.

The company also claimed, in its EIS (2011, p. 42), that all fishpond owners would be compensated, and photos were taken of each owner after the destruction of his ponds. However, according to most of the respondents, nobody had received an indemnification. Many fishpond owners were angry and thought that the chiefs may have received the money but not distributed it to them (see also Schuppli 2016, p. 108). As a result, they planned to take GADCO to court.

> When they started making the canals, we realized they would
> destroy our ponds so we went to confront them and they told us
> they will compensate us for the ponds so we allowed them to do it
> and give us the money. But as they are not giving us the money, we
> have regretted allowing them to use it.
>
> (HH:E2, young man, Fievie-Dugame, 28 June 2014)

Because the majority of land acquired by the company had been used communally, no reimbursement was paid for this land, even though it originally belonged to a specific family. In various informal conversations, different members of this family complained that they felt cheated as no compensation was coming to them and that only one of the grandsons of the family head was employed by the company.

Employment

In the context of high unemployment and high poverty rates, most people initially believed that the GADCO investment would create much-needed employment and development. These aspects were also taken up by the chiefs to make the investment desirable to the people.

> It is a source of employment that came to the community and we were told that if we are employed, there would be a difference between our standard of living and poverty.
> (HH:E2, male former employee, Fievie-Dugame, 28 June 2014)

According to the company's EIS (2011), GADCO estimated that about 25 people, including management staff, agronomists, operators and security personnel, would be permanently employed. Furthermore, it was calculated that up to roughly 200 casual workers would be hired for clearing the land, for fertilizer application and harvesting (EIS, p. 31). At the time of research in 2014, GADCO employed about 120 people on the farm and 30 people in the rice mill, the large majority being men (E4, former GADCO manager, 22 June 2014). According to many conversations with current and former employees, few workers – mostly those working in the rice mill as well as specially qualified agronomists – appeared to have a permanent contract. Whereas most of the full-time employees in the mill were Brazilians, other permanent workers came from nearby bigger towns, such as Sogakope. The majority of the workers were hired on a temporary basis, with appointment letters rather than contracts, or were employed as casual labourers paid daily. Most of the labourers, mechanics, electricians and security guards interviewed earned between 240 and 300 GHS per month, whereas four specially chosen and armed security guards earned 400 GHS and one tractor operator reportedly earned 500 GHS per month (all five were very well connected to the Fievie customary authorities)[2]. All employees who were interviewed were very bitter about the extremely low salaries the company paid. Two employees had quit because of their low salary and another two reported thinking of quitting in the near future.

Workers had founded a union and complained several times to the company about wages. Various people also reported having had work accidents. One woman reported that she was run over by a tractor while working for GADCO – the company apparently did not pay for her hospitalisation, and as a result of the accident, she could not work again. Another man lost his eyesight in one eye because of a battery explosion at GADCO's pump station, where he was working. GADCO paid for his treatment, doubled his salary from 300 to 600 GHS a month and gave him a free bag of rice every month.

Women were hired only as casual labourers for the application of fertilizers and as cooks and cleaners. The justification for this was that it was tedious work, which was better suited to women, and – as the quote below illustrates – the general manager seemed to be aware of the gender stereotypes in his employment policy.

> Most employees are men, like irrigation staff and operators, it's probably a 70%, 30% split. The women do two things: They apply fertilizer, and also logistics, like feeding the farm staff. (...) At least 30 people are employed in the mill, cause they run shifts. There is one female there and she is the cleaner. This doesn't sound good, right?
>
> (E4, Former GADCO manager, Vume, 22 June 2014)

Nine GHS[3] per day were paid for the application of fertilizers, which often was done without adequate protective equipment despite claims in GADCO's EIS that this equipment would be a requirement for anybody involved in the application of agrochemicals. It was also mentioned in one of the community meetings that some of the people who used to work on the farm had been harmed by agrochemicals and now had to stay home because of eye problems. Women who engaged in these tasks came predominantly from poor households and included many young unmarried women, working to supplement their family's income, to finance their own education or to be able to look after their children.

Despite the company's claims to focus on empowering women, its employment practices clearly perpetuated gendered stereotypes that devalued women's labour. Furthermore, there was a strong disparity between the working conditions and salaries of the few educated office and mill workers and the majority of local plantation workers.

Outgrowing

Although GADCO was operating outgrower schemes in Ho, Hohoe, Kpong and Weta, which included about 600 outgrowers in 2014, this study investigated only the local Fievie Connect Scheme, which was directly linked to the company's rice plantation and generally portrayed as part of GADCO's corporate social responsibility to compensate people for the loss of land. It was also the main avenue through which GADCO claimed to empower women.

Under Fievie Connect, local people were trained to farm rice. They were jointly given a 45-ha plot of land on the company's plantation and provided with pesticides, weedicides and fertilizers – the costs of which were deducted from the earnings made at harvest time. The company guaranteed to buy the outgrowers' produce at the Ghanaian market rate at the time of harvest – the money then was divided between all of them according to how often they had been present on the field. However, no contracts were signed with individual outgrowers and all outgrowers were selected by the chiefs without any interference from the company.

At the time of the first field research, the company was thus working with 45 outgrowers (1 ha per person) and a list of names was readily provided. Although only half of the names on the list were female, many more women were visible on the fields. It was frequently mentioned that men who had signed up for the scheme sent their wives to do the work. In some cases, the earnings then were shared between husband and wife; in others, the wife had to hand over the income to her husband.

> The reason that more women are enrolled in the outgrower scheme is that women are more hardworking than men. Some men are also enrolled, but they rather send their wives to do the work.
> (Informal conversation, Paramount Queen Mother, Research Diary 2, 6 July 2016)

As was evident on the outgrower list, the majority of outgrowers came from Fievie-Dugame, where many of the chiefs' relatives lived. No outgrowers from Bakpa Adzani or Kpevikpo were selected, and only one person from Kpodzi (a brother of one of the clan heads promoting the large-scale land acquisition) was selected – although these three settlements were bearing the brunt of the loss of land and resources and also reportedly were heavily affected by the company's aerial spraying of pesticides. When interviews were conducted with 10 randomly selected outgrowers (five men and five women), it became equally clear that the majority of the outgrowers came from chiefs' families or were related to other locally important people, and some families had several positions in the outgrower scheme. Only a few poorer widows had been chosen for the scheme; again, these widows were the ones with good connections to the elite. Furthermore, despite very high unemployment of young men, mostly elderly people were included in the scheme.

> There's a particular house here. The people from that house working on the rice farm are more than those from other families. Why should it be so? Meanwhile, they say the project would benefit people of the community; they did not say it would benefit only a particular family. (…) They said the project would benefit both adults and the youth but if you visit the farm, you would see only old men and women. We the youth were supposed to be working on the farm, but they employed old men and old women, is that good?
>
> (FGD3, young women, Fievie-Dugame, 26 June 2016)

Even though the outgrowers organised themselves in shifts, spending half a day on the outgrower field and half on their own plot, several women reported an increase in their work burden, as outgrowing was simply added to all other productive and reproductive activities and some women reduced the size of their own plots as a result. The increasing time burden, however, was most pronounced for the few poor widows among the outgrowers, those who – unlike many of the richer individuals – could not send labourers to the outgrower fields or hire labourers to take over their own farm work.

In 2016, the company (now under RMG Concept Ltd management) had received money from the Ghana Commercial Agriculture Project (GCAP) to expand the local outgrower scheme by adding 120 outgrowers. However, the integration of an additional 120 ha of land into the company's plantation turned out to be very difficult, as several people mounted heavy resistance, which will be detailed below. According to the GADCO manager, the company also had difficulties finding enough people who were interested in joining the scheme, so at the end of the fieldwork, the number of outgrowers had increased from 45 to only 60 people, who now each worked alone on 1 ha of land (E23, GADCO manager, Sogakope, 6 July 2016).

During the second field research, the company refused to give out the names of any of the outgrowers and also instructed all staff to give us no information. With the help of one individual, however, a partial list of the 15 new outgrowers was collated; again, it was evident that more chiefs had been added to the scheme. Again, it was not clear how many outgrowers in total were women and how many were men (as the names did not match the great number of women seen at work). The official GCAP criterion was that at least 40% of outgrowers must be female, but obviously women were outnumbering the men.

All outgrowers interviewed during the first research period had been happy to be included in the outgrower scheme, as they perceived it to be much more profitable and less prone to harvest failure as their own rainfed farming. The income mentioned ranged from 1700 to 3000 GHS per harvest[4]. However, one of the reasons for the lack of interest in the expansion of the scheme – witnessed during the second research period – was the fact that, in 2015, a large part of the crop was spoiled by heavy rains and the harvest was impeded by the breakdown of the company's harvesters. This meant that most outgrowers had received very little money (i.e. 800 GHS). Many of the previously enthusiastic participants had become disillusioned with the scheme as a result of the harvest failure.

> Some people had two harvests, but we had it once. (…) The previous one was when the company went bankrupt, so some of us were given GHC 800 – 900. (…) I am happy to be an outgrower, but with regards to payments I am not very happy, because it's our workplace that they have destroyed, our farmlands that they have taken. The rice farm has come so we expect to make some money from there.
>
> (E18, female outgrower representative, Fievie-Dugame,
> 1 May 2016)

Both the chiefs and the company management had noticed that the majority of those who signed up for the scheme did not work on the fields themselves but rather hired labourers to work on the outgrower fields for them (or, in the case of male married participants, sent their wives). Although the company manager attributed this to the general "laziness" of Ghanaian men, it was evident that most of the outgrowers, being wealthy and pursuing several income-earning activities, simply did not have the time or did not feel the necessity to work on the fields themselves.

It became clear during the first research that, from the company's point of view, the outgrower scheme was very profitable, as the harvest achieved by outgrowers surpassed that of the plantation (E13, GADCO Production Manager, Sogakope, 15 April 2014). However, all risks of harvest failure were shifted to the outgrowers, who became heavily dependent on the company, its equipment and its timing for the harvest. Many outgrowers thus complained that the major harvests were always in the rainy season, making it difficult for the tractors to move through the fields. During an informal conversation, some men mentioned that many times they had asked the company as well as the chiefs to move the harvesting to the dry season but were ignored (Research Diary 2, 26 June 2016).

Access to infrastructure

GADCO's EIS (2011, p. 31) states that

> the infrastructure that GADCO would develop offers the opportunity to boost their [smallholders] production and income. For example, the canals and water infrastructure developed will bring irrigation infrastructure to parts of the land that has never been irrigated. This offers the opportunity for local farmers to work with GADCO to support local farming activities through this shared infrastructure.

Similarly, the revised EMP (2015, p. 16) states that the company

> has carried out several social actions to develop the living conditions of nearby communities. Indeed, the company maintains some local infrastructure, specifically, the rough road between Fievie and Kpevikpo, the bridge on it and all dams built by GADCO (Agorkpo, Agorkpoenu, Awusekpoe, Kortortsikope, Dendo, Avorvi, Kpevikpo, Kpodzi).

During both the 2014 and 2016 research, irrigation infrastructure was not shared but rather just used to water the company's and the outgrowers' fields. The dams that were mentioned above mainly had the purpose of preventing flooding of the fields and keeping the water inside the canals. These were actually a particular nuisance to local people, as during the rainy season the roads were frequently flooded because water could not drain into the company's fields. In the case of Kpevikpo, this was made even worse by the fact that GADCO had built a canal right outside the village. Even though the company had expanded the small footpath that previously linked Kpevikpo to other villages and had turned it into a rough road, thus making the village more accessible, the canal heavily constrained accessibility to the village during the rainy season and during irrigation times. Whenever the company irrigated its fields or when there were heavy rains, people from Kpevikpo could leave their village only by wading through chest-deep water and children could not leave the village at all. As a result, they could not attend school whenever the canal was flooded. The bridge that the company claimed to have built consisted simply of a few low-lying bricks inside the canal and did not improve the situation.

> How the road was before they came, we could move on it freely without any worries, but now the construction of the canal, with a little mistake, the water can carry you away so that is why we blame them. Our lives are now threatened. (…) I have not identified any positive benefit we derived from the coming of GADCO. They only destroyed our properties. The road, if it had rained, you would not be able to come here. We kept asking them to make a small bridge over the canal too, they refused to do it.
>
> (B16, middle-aged woman, Kpevikpo, 1 May 2016)

Resistance to the investment

Although some people initially approached the company to stop them from entering their farmland or to demand compensation, they were generally referred to the traditional authorities. The villagers thus quickly realised that the traditional authorities had granted the company access to the land and that they had to negotiate with their chiefs in order to receive compensation or address any other grievances.

Apart from some individual acts of violence and resistance, most women and men from within the Fievie Traditional Area first tried to approach their chiefs and use traditional means of dispute settlement to voice their complaints and ask for compensation. However, they were usually referred to other members of the "community liaison committee" or asked to come back another time.

Many community meetings were held to discuss various issues related to the GADCO plantation, such as the loss of farmland, the loss of grazing land, fishponds and fuelwood as well as the destruction of water ponds and the spraying of pesticides. However, as the meetings continued, it became clear that decisions had already been taken. People usually addressed chiefs very politely in these meetings, but as time passed, frustration with chiefs was rising, meetings became more and more agitated, and many people started coming late to meetings or stopped attending them altogether.

> We have tried several times but did not succeed so we gave up. Because when you say anything, they would not consider it. So, we think it's better to keep mute. (…) We all attended meetings, but

what happens is that whatever you tell them, they would not listen. Only some two or three chiefs would sit somewhere and decide otherwise. That's why when they call community meetings we don't go anymore because whatever you contribute would not be used.
(FGD4, young men, Fievie-Dugame, 26 June 2016)

Involvement of the government

Several people complained to the DCEs, District Directorates of Agriculture and individual members of parliament (MPs) about the loss of land without compensation, the aerial spraying of pesticides, and the construction of the canal near Kpevikpo.

Some communities have come complaining that any time it rains, the various canals that they [GADCO] have created, when it over-rains, the water overfloods its banks and spills into their communities. They even called me on two occasions to go see some of the issues. That was the formal complaint I've received, other than that, it's just the normal complaints that, well the farms are all around us, now we don't have access to our old farmlands, and all that. But it is our traditional authorities who negotiated this and said this people are settlers on the land and so they were supposed to have consulted them.
(E5b, DCE, Sogakope, 23 May 2016)

The quote above highlights the ability of customary authorities to redefine customary use rights. By labelling certain people as mere "settlers", customary authorities effectively disenfranchised these people, even in the eyes of government authorities, who did not follow up claims of land loss of settlers. Generally, even though various government representatives were approached about the issues, nothing was done about it.

The assembly member, the MP, the DCE and Zikpuitor [Stoolfather] are all aware. Even the recent flooding, the assembly member and the MP came and inspected it. The secretary for the outgrowers was also involved (...) They said they would do something about it but they have not done anything yet.
(HH:E6, former security guard, Kpevikpo, 28 June 2014)

Cattle herders formed a committee headed by the leader of the cattle herders union and sent a letter to the DCE, the elders and the company, asking them to address the negative effects of spraying, the destruction of water ponds, the impacts of the canal, and the flooding of the road to Kpevikpo. The letter further expressed their resistance to the appropriation of an additional 120 ha of grazing land for the expansion of the outgrower scheme. The herders also involved an MP and the local media. However, they never received a reply to their letter. At the time of the first research, they were also considering taking their complaints to the regional or even the national government level.

But, as has been mentioned, various government officials appeared keen to portray GADCO as a best practice example and even the vice president of Ghana pledged his support to the company. Moreover, the company and the traditional authorities had good connections with key political figures, which may be one of the reasons the herders' protest has shown little results.

Court cases

None of the individuals interviewed mentioned having engaged in a court case as a result of losing land to GADCO. There were various reasons for not going to court: on the one hand, once people realised that their chiefs had given the land out to the company, they rather negotiated with their chiefs. To engage in a court case against one's own chiefs would have been very problematic as chiefs still enjoyed great respect. On the other hand, litigation was very expensive and time-consuming, making it unaffordable to most people. However, at two community meetings, two individuals mentioned having gone to court against GADCO but with no results.

> I am from Kpevikpo. This is my father's land. When GADCO came, they took our land. We litigated but nothing came out of it. When the outgrower project came, no one from my family benefitted.
> (Woman at community meeting, Fievie-Dugame, 24 May 2014)

The biggest court case that ensued as a result of the GADCO acquisition related to Bakpa land. Bakpa people, together with a family from Adidome, were already locked in a court case against Fievie because of the previous land acquisition by Galten Ltd. Once GADCO entered their land, a new plaint was added to the ongoing court case in order to resolve once and for all who was the rightful owner of all Bakpa land. If the court would establish that Bakpa land had originally been provided by the Mafi Traditional Area, the land used by GADCO would automatically revert to the Bakpa people. However, according to various interviews with Bakpa chiefs, the court case was continually postponed by Fievie chiefs, who either did not show up to hearings or, as was suspected by Bakpa, paid the judges to keep delaying the case.

> You know Ghana with its legal issues, they don't go straight; they go and come back. But we know that they [Fievie chiefs] take money from the investor and are influencing to prolong the issues because they have the financial power to influence.
>
> (FGD5, Bakpa elders and youth, Bakpa Adzani, 6 July 2016)

Another group that considered taking GADCO to court were the fishpond owners, who had been promised compensation for the destruction of their ponds but after four years had still not received anything. As has been highlighted by Schuppli (2016, p. 105), fishpond owners were planning action – against the explicit wishes of their chiefs, who tried to dissuade them from going to court.

> Today we have to take action against GADCO because they cannot come and destroy our ponds without paying even a penny to anybody. So, we have decided to go to court. We have to take GADCO to court for compensation. (…) We can no longer listen to the elders anymore.
>
> (Household Interview, fishpond owner, Fievie-Dugame, 3 March 2015, *DS)

Individual acts of resistance and violence

There were many incidences of people showing their resentment by stealing both rice from GADCO's fields and fuel from their machines. These issues were frequently discussed at community meetings where the chiefs told people to stop stealing from the company. Several incidences of violence were also reported as a result of the GADCO acquisition. Initially, many individual farmers whose land was enclosed by the plantation without warning took up arms and threatened the company representatives with violence. Others continually pulled out the demarcations that the company had put on their land. Yet others destroyed some of the company's machinery (Research Diary 1, 5 May 2014).

At the time of the first research, as the company was planning to expand its outgrower scheme, several physical fights were also reported and death threats were issued. An informal conversation with the GADCO manager also revealed the increasing number of threats and violence related to the land acquisition. He complained that there had been many incidences and threats since the project started but nothing ever happened. He himself had also received death threats but thought that it was all hot air. He mentioned how one of the youth leaders once came with a big knife, with which he pretended to slit his own throat, saying he would kill him. Then he pointed out that now this youth leader was his best friend (Research Diary 1, 20 May 2014).

However, these individual acts of resistance were met by the company with an increase in security measures, including four specially armed security guards chosen by the customary authorities. Furthermore, it became clear that selected individuals were provided with compensation or a position in the company's outgrower scheme (or both) as a way to mute their resistance. For example, the youth leader mentioned in the diary entrance above not only received compensation but also was selected to be an outgrower and was in the process of building a new house. In fact, several of the interviewees who apparently were initially resisting the investment were at the time of research heavily supporting the investment and several of them were constructing new houses.

Similarly, the cattle rearer representative who was quoted above and in 2014 was a leading figure in the resistance of the cattle herders had become an outgrower during the second field research and by then was strongly in support of GADCO (Research Diary 2, 29 April 2016). Initially, he was emotionally contesting the expansion of the investment at many community meetings, but from one meeting to the next he turned into a fervent supporter of the acquisition. According to some cattle rearers, more and more people were bought off, thus making their resistance vanish.

> In every community there was a representative. So, if in your community, you are cattle herder and you are selected to represent your community, you may turn to team up with the GADCO Company. So in this small, small way, the union executives turned to go to the side of GADCO.
>
> (Household interview, cattle herder, Kpevikpo, 12 February 2015, *DS)

Organised violence

Bakpa farmers whose land was enclosed without consultation or compensation also initially turned to violence. Several men armed themselves and occupied their land, threatening to kill anybody who would come near. This standoff led to an intervention by the District Security Councils of North and South Tongu, which called a meeting with Fievie and Bakpa chiefs and GADCO. As a result, an independent evaluation of the loss of land and the compensation to be paid by GADCO was carried out. As highlighted before, GADCO, however, compensated only 9 out of 26 affected farmers, creating a lot of conflict and resentment within the community. Whenever Bakpa farmers continued using some of the land that had been acquired by GADCO but was not yet used by the company, they were attacked by a group of Fievie youth.

> This season when we were ploughing to plant our pepper, a mob from Fievie came and attacked us including our chief. They were in a KIA truck, came and heckled, buckled us out of the farm physically. A report was made to the Police and records are there to show.
> (HH:L5, middle-aged man, Bakpa Adzani, 13 June 2014)

This was confirmed by several other interviewees, including the Paramount Stoolfather and the former GADCO manager, who confirmed that whenever there was a problem (i.e. when people were "illegally ploughing" their land), the company provided a pick-up truck to the chiefs, who then organised the local youth to go and combat these people (E14a, Stoolfather, 24 May 2014; Research Diary 1, 5 May 2014). Although Fievie chiefs also used community meetings to incite people against the Bakpa community, there were indications that some Fievie youth were not happy with the situation anymore and refused to give respect to their elders.

> They [Bakpa people] were given land by our grandfathers to resettle, but as they expand the GADCO farm to their side, they are showing resistance. That is why the elders will send us to go and reclaim those lands. (…) we've been going with guns and clubs and they also come with the same but we never clashed. (…) They don't pay us for that. When anything is suspected, the farm people call Zikpuitor and he will also call and instruct us to go and fight those people. Later when they come, they don't invite us to let us know about who the actual owner of the property is. They only call meetings without us and before we realize, they are gone.
> (HH:E2, young man, Fievie-Dugame, 28 June 2014)

Whereas Bakpa youth wanted to violently retaliate against Fievie, the Bakpa elders persuaded them during several community meetings to be patient and wait for the resolution of the ongoing court case, to which the GADCO land acquisition had been added. According to a member of the Bakpa Traditional Council, "the elders did not want violence, as they knew that there would be dead people, and they did not want to be in the news for such a thing" (Research Diary 1, 13 June 2014).

Gendered resistance?

Interestingly, no women appeared to be engaged in any of the above-mentioned resistance strategies. Though voicing the concerns of both women and men, both the cattle herder group and the group of Bakpas who engaged in violence were dominated by men. On the one hand, since most land belonged to men, women felt they could not contest the loss of land. On the other hand, violence and direct confrontation are related to prevalent notions of masculinity and women considered themselves to be "weak".

Furthermore, women tended to have less voice in the customary system and thus less influence on traditional leaders. However, there were notable exceptions, such as a very influential local Queen Mother from the clan of the Paramount Stoolfather as well as a female ex–Assembly member, who were both members of the committee dealing with the GADCO community development fund. Another reason why women were less engaged in resistance was their heavy workload and the fact that they were responsible for providing food to their families. Thus, they quickly had to find ways to cope with the loss of land and resources in order to ensure their family's food security.

Adaptation strategies

The fact that many people lost access to land and resources without compensation put poorer people (whose families did not have large land holdings) in a difficult situation. Although there were still large tracts of land available for the expansion of farming activities within the Fievie Traditional Area, most of the remaining farmland near Bakpa Adzani was already in use. In all villages, some wealthier women and men could get access to new farmland through their families, but respondents, especially in Bakpa Adzani, mentioned that only very little land was available and even for those who could get access to family land, farming activities had regressed drastically.

In all study villages, several respondents, especially women, reported having to resort to sharecropping or to leasing land. This can be seen as an indication that in families where land was scarce, men were given preference for access to new land at the expense of women.

In Kpodzi and Kpevikpo, many new tracts of bushland which previously had been used for grazing and the collection of fuelwoods were cleared for farming. As has been highlighted by Schuppli's study (2015, p. 89), "many farmers acquired new farmland through either cultivating fallow family lands, or through acquiring virgin plots". His study, in particular, points out the situation of Kpodzi, which lost large tracts of farmland to GADCO and as a result cleared large new areas of bushland. As a consequence, around 190 ha of formerly jointly used areas were converted into farmland, further reducing areas available for grazing and for collecting fuelwoods (Schuppli 2016, p. 90).

Thus, most people somehow were able to get access to new farmland (through cultivating fallow family land, clearing new farmland or sharecropping), but in most cases, the new fields were much smaller than the ones previously cultivated. Furthermore, many respondents mentioned changing their farming practices and the crop variety in order to adapt to the new situation.

Several employees also mentioned having neglected the farm work on their own fields as a result of their employment. In some cases, they reduced their farming activities or stopped them altogether; in other cases, they hired labourers or shifted farm work to their wives, thus increasing the burden of work of these women.

> I wake up early to go to my farm before reporting at the GADCO fields but it makes me feel so tired and the salary I take from there is so meager that I cannot give my wife anything when my wife alone is working on our farm now. That's why I have decided not to work for GADCO anymore.
>
> (HH:E2, former employee, Fievie-Dugame, 28 June 2014)

Even though most people managed to access new land for farming, the majority of those who lost land, as well as employees and outgrowers, reported increasingly purchasing food for household consumption.

> We took more from the farm than we bought. The only thing we bought is cooking oil and fish, but now we buy everything.
>
> (HH:LL2, elderly widow, Bakpa Adzani, 13 June 2014)

Coping with the reduction in grazing areas

Most of the land used by GADCO was previously used for grazing livestock. At the same time, the above-mentioned cultivation of new farmlands further reduced the area of grazing land available to cattle herders (see Schuppli 2016, p. 110). In particular, the loss of floodplain areas for dry-season grazing caused fodder shortages in the dry season. The continued grazing on the areas not yet converted into a rice field led to a perceptible degradation of the quality of pasture.

Not only the loss of grazing land posed a problem to cattle owners. The destruction of water ponds and the deterioration of the water quality in the remaining ponds, both a result of GADCO's use of pesticides and fertilizers, were also major worries of many cattle owners. As cattle rearing was becoming more difficult, some cattle owners reported selling some or all of their cows and others mentioned increasingly grazing their cattle in bordering traditional areas. Because cattle herders generally had good relationships with each other and also were organised in a Regional Union, herding across boundaries was usually unproblematic. However, one cattle rearer mentioned that nowadays they were sometimes asked to pay to use pasture in the Mafi Traditional Area.

As cattle owners were most vocally resisting the expansion of the GADCO plantation, the traditional authorities were also keen to find a solution to the problems. At various community meetings, they tried to persuade cattle owners to switch to intensive livestock grazing practices (i.e. to keep cattle confined and produce hay for fodder instead of letting livestock graze). Whereas a few people showed an interest in trying to adopt new methods for cattle rearing, the majority of herders were suspicious and did not want to change their practices.

Coping with the loss of fishponds

The loss of fishponds was a big worry for many people, as fish was a crucial part of their diet. Various villagers mentioned now having to buy fish.

> Nothing has changed with the way we eat food, just that the variety of foods which are produced and eaten have changed. Like tomatoes, okro, garden eggs are no more available, and the fish, – we are suffering a lot. Because in those times I also went fishing myself using the nets. But now if we don't buy fish, we would not eat fish.
>
> (B15, middle-aged woman, Kpevikpo, 1 May 2016)

Some people nevertheless had adapted to the new reality by fishing in the GADCO canals, even though the water was contaminated and the quality of the fish was much lower than before. However, unlike the fish harvesting, which took place in fishponds and used simple methods, fishing in the canal required special skills and equipment. Schuppli (2016, p. 108) describes how formerly anybody could catch fish in the floodplains during the rainy seasons and fishpond owners could manually collect fish in the ponds during the dry season. Because the canals are much deeper than the ponds, people now needed nets or hooks to fish and many were afraid to go close to the canal, as the water was very deep and they could not swim.

Coping with the loss of water and fuelwood

The loss of water and fuelwood affected women disproportionately, as they were the ones in charge of collecting both water and fuelwood and many also sold firewood and charcoal for a living. People from Fievie-Dugame, Kpodzi and Kpevikpo all relied at least partly on water from ponds for their own consumption or to water their animals (or both). Most respondents from Fievie-Dugame mentioned getting water from the river now and those from Kpodzi could use the water tap at the nearby Red Bull Soccer Academy for their own consumption but were affected by the lack of watering opportunities for their cattle. In Kpevikpo, however, people were affected simultaneously by the destruction of water ponds and the building of a canal through their access road, often making the village inaccessible. Although women walked to the Red Bull Soccer Academy to collect water or went to buy drinking water, these options were not available when the canal was flooded. GADCO had installed a polytank in the village, but it was filled up only a few times. Many people in Kpevikpo reported using water from the canal for bathing and cooking, and several reported having been ill as a result of the chemicals in the water. They had also started to harvest rainwater to cope with the water shortage.

> They [GADCO] destroyed our source of drinking water and if they have not opened the irrigation into the rice seedling, we wouldn't get any water to drink. But now we are not drinking it and only bathing with it and we are noticing that the chemicals they spray in the farm are going into the water so it may affect us but because we don't get any other source of water we keep on using it.
>
> (B16, middle-aged woman, Kpevikpo, 1 May 2016)

The destruction of trees not only made fuelwood/charcoal selling an unviable activity but also led to the destruction of remaining trees, as women cut them down for firewood for their own household. Most women, however, managed to at least partly offset the losses incurred from not being able to sell fuelwood by gleaning rice from the company's plantation after every harvest.

Gleaning of rice

A major way of coping with the many losses inflicted by the GADCO investment, especially for women, was the gleaning of rice, which started right after the company's first harvest, when many women went to the rice fields to collect the leftover rice grains that the company's combined harvesters could not collect. Although the company first wanted to prohibit this practice, some women asked their chiefs for support and finally were allowed to continue gleaning the leftovers. At the time of research, hundreds of women from many different villages could be seen on the rice fields gleaning rice, and both the company and chiefs used this strenuous work to praise the benefits of the investment to the local communities.

> [The rice picking] is something that happened and we decided to not intervene. Basically, when we are harvesting, the harvester does not pick up all the rice. What other farms do is that they let the women harvest, but at the end of it they take a proportion of their bags and let them have the rest. But we decided just to let them have everything when the harvester has gone off the field.
>
> (E4, former GADCO manager, Vume, 22 June 2014)

The majority of all interviewees had some female household members who were gleaning rice and all of them agreed that this arduous work had positive consequences for their household, especially in terms of availability of food. However, it soon became clear that for many women, gleaning rice was also a strategy to cope with the losses related to the investment.

> Since they [the company] have destroyed all these things and we have used the gleaning of the rice to compensate those losses, we were happy about it. But just that it did not keep long when they stopped farming on the field and now it has caused a lot of burden on us again. At first, the gleaning of rice compared to the losses, it was somehow better but now that they have stopped, the burden is felt again. (…) They have destroyed everything and uprooted the trees with their stumps so the trees are not able to grow again. Even as they have stopped their operations it is not possible to get firewood or other resources from the land again.
>
> (Focus Group, rice pickers, Fievie-Dugame, 16 March 2015, *ES)

Although many women of all ages were working on the rice fields, those profiting most were the ones who had many children to help as well as the outgrowers who could pick the leftovers from their own fields or ask poorer community members to pick the grains for them and then divide the share (2/3 for the outgrower and 1/3 for the picker). The majority of women who reported making an income from rice gleaning mentioned that they kept the money and used it to buy food for the family. The reported incomes from this activity ranged from 100 to 400 GHS[5] per month, depending on the number of days and hours spent on the fields.

Many women mentioned that they did not like gleaning rice, as it was very strenuous and the proceeds from it were limited, but no other options were available to them. Furthermore, owing to the ongoing court case, only a few people from Bakpa reported engaging in the rice picking.

> I may say it has not brought any opportunities for us but rather came to spoil our things. Nobody from here is employed. Our women and children don't pick rice from there because they have destroyed our things and we are litigating with them so we don't allow our children to go there.
>
> (B4, middle-aged man, Bakpa Adzani, 25 June 2016)

However, as a result of the practice of rice gleaning, the general availability of rice in the local area had greatly increased and rice had become more affordable to many families. A local rice mill had also been established near Kpevikpo, where the women could bring their rice to be milled before consuming or selling it. A clear change in consumption patterns was evident, as many people reported eating less of their traditional food and eating more rice.

Though certainly helping to offset the losses for many families, the gleaning of rice at the same time increased people's dependency on the company for their livelihoods and their food security. It is also telling that only women engaged in this activity; on the one hand, it reflects women's care burden, as they were generally in charge of providing food to the family; on the other hand, it mirrors the nature of the work itself, which men saw as too degrading and not profitable enough for them to engage in. As one woman mentioned:

> Few men come, but they think it is a woman's job and they would be laughed at if they would do it.
>
> (Informal conversation with rice pickers on the field,
> Research Diary 1, 17 June 2014)

Outlook

The research has shown a very dynamic context and changing land relations. GADCO has entered the Fievie Traditional Area at a time of rising values of land and increased investor interest. Through the Customary Land Secretariat, some chiefs have managed to increase their power and to change the land tenure system in their favour. The case study has highlighted that chiefs and their relatives have predominantly benefited from the investment. At the same time, it has been shown that different land users have resisted the investment and found ways to adapt to it.

GADCO's proclaimed aim was to expand the farm to 5000 ha minimum, employ 5000 outgrowers – including those already working in other areas of Ghana – and process 50,000 tons of rice and create partnerships with different communities all over the country (Rice Mill Opening Ceremony, 9 April 2014). It was not clear whether the follow-up (and current) company still had the same goals, but during the second research period, the new manager mentioned that they planned to expand to at least the 2500 ha covered in the lease document (E23, GADCO manager, 6 July 2016). An expansion of the investment seemed in the interest of many of the customary authorities who were benefiting from land sales.

> But we, let me tell you, we don't see the wisdom of continuing with the traditional crops again. Because when you look at the use of rice as compared to them, it is more. Because you can sell your rice to buy your traditional crops. The yield from a hectare of rice is enormous, so 5000 GHC every harvest, you cannot get that from cassava. One hectare of cassava or maize cannot give you the same yield, you see. And rice, because it is under irrigation, every 4 months, a ready market. So, to us, or to me, there is a need, let us all go into rice cultivation.
>
> (E14a, Paramount Stoolfather, Sogakope, 24 May 2014)

Although it is unlikely that everybody would "go into rice cultivation", as the Stoolfather suggested, any expansion of the plantation would obviously have tremendous consequences for the local communities. The following paragraphs will first discuss the various effects such an expansion might have, before outlining what might happen if the new company again went bankrupt, which – given the many failed investments in Ghana – is also an imaginable scenario. Lastly, an alternative scenario will be discussed in which local people through resistance and possibly even destoolment of the current chiefs might manage to get a better deal out of the company.

Scenario 1: Expansion of the investment

Most likely, the expansion of the rice farm would cover all of the remaining grazing land and make it impossible for cattle rearers to continue with their livelihood. Throughout the research, it became clear that the customary authorities did not see the need for cattle rearing anymore. They variously described the activity as backwards and tried to persuade livestock farmers to adopt intensive livestock farming methods. In an interview, the Paramount Stoolfather confirmed that they were planning to take the remaining grazing land for the expansion of GADCO.

> You see how they are struggling, the cattle owners. Anytime we come, they sit as a group, because they know that their livelihood is threatened. We can take it, it is not their land, they are licensees. Now the community needs the land, because we are looking at the greater benefit to the greatest number of people. (…) If it is not taken today, tomorrow we shall take it. They know. We have it in view, we have that land in view.
>
> (E14a, Paramount Stoolfather, Sogakope, 24 May 2014)

Furthermore, most likely, the whole settlement of Kpevikpo would be moved to a different location, as it is already surrounded by the rice farm and after an expansion, the village would be trapped right in the middle of the plantation. This would certainly lead to renewed conflicts and resistance and possibly even violence. Some livestock farmers might be persuaded to adopt intensive livestock farming methods; others might be placated by compensation payments or positions in the outgrower scheme (or both). However, the poorest and the least well-connected people likely will bear the brunt of the conversion of grazing land into a rice farm.

Increased land scarcity

At the time of the second research, there was still land available for the expansion of farming. It was concentrated in the hands of a few families, and others had to resort to sharecropping. With the enlargement of the GADCO plantation, large parts of this land would be gone, thus severely limiting the possibility of expanding individual farming activities and sharecropping as well as limiting the availability of new farmland for future generations.

Although the Paramount Stoolfather also foresaw this scenario, he seemed to believe that those losing land would be absorbed by the rice farm as outgrowers, which is highly unlikely. First, it was not clear how much land would be allocated for the outgrower scheme and how much would be integrated into the highly mechanised plantation. Given the fact that most outgrowers so far were relatives of the chiefs, it is secondly most probable that again mainly the elite would benefit from an expansion of the plantation and of the outgrower scheme.

The resulting land scarcity, however, would have the biggest impact on the poorest members of society, especially women, whose land rights under customary tenure are much less secure than men's. Again, there would certainly be resistance and compensation would have to be paid in order to get people's consent. Increased migration might be a result of such land scarcity.

Poverty and loss of livelihood for the Bakpa people

It is also likely that the plantation would reach the two Bakpa settlements. The former GADCO manager confirmed that their contract also covered the land that was previously used by Galten Ltd., and at the time of research, there was still an injunction on it. GADCO would not be able to enter the land until the court reached a decision, but if that decision turns out to be in favour of Fievie, both Bakpa settlements would likely be surrounded by the plantation.

> There is no more new land, since all was sold to the GADCO Company. Even our houses here too. They are saying they will break down our houses and farm here. We are only waiting for them to come and break them down for us to be free. (…) there is no hope for the future since they are just continuing what they are doing so we don't cast our minds on them again. There is nothing to pick from the land anymore, not even trees for fuelwoods so I am just thinking to migrate to the Northern Region where there are lot of vast land idle.
> (B1, middle-aged woman, Bakpa Adzani, 21 May 2016)

As pointed out in the quote above, some people in Bakpa were already considering migration at the time of research. Although the elders were waiting for the court case to be resolved in their favour, it is likely that if this were not the case, there would be violence, which might even lead to the downfall of the company.

Scenario 2: Possible bankruptcy of the company

Given the fact that GADCO went bankrupt after only four years, there is no guarantee that the new company will stay in the area for long.

Many of my respondents were convinced that the company was on the ground only to make money and that once they had accumulated enough profit, they might withdraw, leaving the land bare and depleted.

Initially, a bankruptcy of the company would certainly leave the people worse off than they were with the company in place. On the one hand, all jobs and outgrower positions would be lost. On the other hand, the gleaning of rice, on which many women have come to depend for food and income, would be gone. All of the resources that were previously on the land, such as fuelwood and fishponds, would already have been destroyed, and by the time of a possible bankruptcy, many cattle rearers might already have sold their cows. Although people would again try to adapt to the new situation, possibly digging new fishponds or trying new farming techniques, their resilience would likely decrease, leaving many families vulnerable to poverty and hunger.

Scenario 3: Successful resistance

During the first research in 2014, most people still expected that the investment could provide them with employment or outgrowing opportunities or would create some infrastructural development in the community through the community development fund. However, during the second field research in 2016, after the new company had taken over, most villagers – even those previously very optimistic – had become deeply disillusioned with the company and did not believe it would bring anything positive anymore. Many aggrieved parties also questioned the content of the contract and wondered whether it had been legal for GADCO to hand over operations to another company. (This issue was discussed at length during the final research dissemination meeting, 6 July 2016.)

However, after the completion of the field research, Fievie youth were coming together to demand accountability from their chiefs. They were even discussing destoolment of some chiefs. However, even if this plan were carried through, it seems improbable that a change in chieftaincy would significantly improve the situation, as a whole group of chiefs and their family members were benefiting from GADCO. Most likely, any destooled chief would be succeeded by one of his family members, who would continue business as usual.

However, the more united the local people are, the more likely that organised – and possibly violent – demonstrations are going to take place, especially if the company expands its operations. Vehement resistance could make it impossible for the chiefs to bribe enough people and thus for the company to continue their operation as before.

The chiefs as well as the company representatives might then be forced to negotiate with the different user groups and not only pay meaningful compensation but also find innovative ways to integrate the affected communities into the company's operations and decision processes and help them to establish alternative livelihoods. Ideally, an external person (i.e. a government official, a non-governmental organisation representative or a researcher) would have to take part in these negotiations to ensure that the voices of the most vulnerable community members – such as women, poor people and settlers – are heard. (See the constitutionality approach of Haller et al. (2016).)

Notes

1 400 GHS equaled USD $140 in May 2014 (on the day of the interview, 24 June 2016, 400 GHS were worth only USD $97).
2 250 GHS equaled USD $87 in May 2014 (source: www.oanda.com).
3 9 GHS equaled USD $3 in May 2014 (source: www.oanda.com).
4 This was equivalent of USD $597–$1053 in 2014 (source: www.oanda. com).
5 100 GHS was equivalent to USD $31, 400 GHS equaled USD $124 (source: www.oanda.com).

References

Barnes, K. (1964). *A study of financial and economic consequences of Ghana Volta River Project part one: Existent rural economy of the inundated Volta Basin*. Accra, Ghana: The State Publishing Corporation.

Haller, T., Acciaioli, G. and S. Rist (2016). 'Constitutionality: Conditions for crafting local ownership of institution-building processes'. *Society & Natural Resources* 29 (1): 68–87.

Moxon, J. (1984). *Volta: Man's greatest lake*. London: Andre Deutsch.

Nyendu, M. (2006). *Enhancing the participation of traditional authorities (chiefs) in Ghana's democratic decentralization programme: A case study of the South Tongu District Assembly of the Volta Region*. PhD dissertation, Calgary, AB: University of Calgary.

Schuppli, D. (2016). *The impact of large-scale land acquisitions on land use and local actor's access to land*. MA thesis, Berne, Switzerland: University of Berne.

Tsikata, D. (2012). *Living in the shadow of the large dam*. Accra, Ghana: Woeli Publishing Services.

6   Conclusion
Contested land deals, gendered power relations

This book has examined how a large-scale land acquisition (LSLA) for rice production has been implemented in the plural legal setting of Ghana, how different actors have been affected by the investment and how they have resisted and adapted to the changed circumstances. It has shown that the social context in the study communities prior to the arrival of Global Agri-Development Company (GADCO) was dynamic and permeated by manifold intersectionally gendered power relations and how unequal power structures have been reinforced rather than reduced by the investment despite the company's claims of sustainability, poverty reduction and "women's empowerment". This chapter will discuss the findings of the case study in light of the theoretical framework outlined in Chapter 1, which posits a relationship between the (inter)national policy context and local institutional change. According to Ensminger's adapted framework of institutional change, the factor that connects the (inter)national policy context and its legitimating ideologies to the local level is the rising relative price of land. These are evidenced locally in the form of increased investor interest in land, leading to LSLAs. In other words, the LSLA serves as a vector through which (inter)national institutions and legitimation strategies are activated and become relevant in the local context. (Inter)national policies and related legitimating ideologies, discourses and narratives are used by different local actors to increase their bargaining power and to shape the distributional effects of institutional change through performing "institution shopping". So I will identify six key findings that emerge from the case study, before outlining some concrete policy recommendations and recommendations for further research.

1. **(Inter)national legitimating discourses and narratives (based on the ideology of modernisation) are used to legitimise policies promoting LSLAs for commercial agriculture. Through the LSLA, which is an**

DOI: 10.4324/9781003212768-6

effect of rising relative prices of land, these discourses and narratives enter the local context, where they are used by powerful actors to legitimise the de facto shift from common to private property.

Chapter 2 showed how international public–private partnerships for the promotion of commercial agriculture in Africa (i.e. the New Alliance for Food Security and Nutrition, the Alliance for a Green Revolution in Africa or the Millennium Challenge Corporation) make use of powerful discourses and narratives that associate commercial agriculture with development and poverty reduction and increasingly also with women's empowerment (all of which are aspects of the broader ideology of modernisation). The same holds true for prevailing land-titling initiatives. Although the focus of international development actors – mirrored in Ghanaian land policies – has shifted from titling private land to supporting customary systems of land tenure, the legitimating ideology of modernisation has remained the same. Common discourses emphasise that clear land rights (whether private or controlled by a customary authority) will increase land tenure security of poor and marginalised community members (especially women) and allow them to invest in their land, thus leading to general development and economic growth.

At the same time, these legitimating discourses serve as an "anti-politics" machine (Ferguson 1994). Whereas Ferguson (1994) has shown how different discourses related to development and modernisation lead to a depoliticisation of development and a strengthening of bureaucratic state power, I argue – based on my case study – that in the current globalised age, it is not necessarily state power, but rather corporate power, that is strengthened by the discourses and narratives outlined above. In Chapter 2, I showed how since the era of structural adjustment, African state policy has been geared towards facilitating the activities of transnational corporations and private investors (see Ferguson 2006; Hoogvelt 1997). It has been pointed out that international donor agencies in close alliance with corporate actors – including, more recently, the New Alliance for Food Security and Nutrition – have hugely influenced Ghanaian agricultural and land policy. Internationally manufactured legitimating discourses used by donor agencies – highlighting the potential of commercial agriculture to reduce poverty, bring development and empower women – are thus also found in Ghanaian policy documents (i.e. FASDEP [Food and Agriculture Sector Development Policy] II and METASIP [Medium-Term Agriculture Sector Investment Plan]) and projects (i.e. the Land Administration Project [LAP]). The use of gender rhetoric is a particularly effective means of legitimation, as has also been emphasised by Roberts (2015, p. 3):

The instrumental use of gender equality by corporations (and their various partners in the public sector and civil society) [...] has become a deeply useful means of reaching new markets and new sources of profitability as well as legitimizing and depoliticizing the exercise of private power.

This has been rather evident with GADCO, which, alongside prominent discourses related to sustainability and poverty reduction, also made use of (inter)nationally manufactured discourses and narratives related to women's empowerment and thereby managed to attract more than USD $20 million in funding from different funding bodies.

Through the GADCO LSLA, which is an outcome of the favourable international policy environment and rising relative prices of land, these legitimating discourses and narratives have also entered the local context, where they were used by customary authorities to advocate the investment towards the local population. It has been shown in previous chapters that many community meetings related to the GADCO land acquisition were used by chiefs to emphasise the LSLA's development potential and that the specific benefits for women were regularly mentioned. Customary authorities often pointed out that, prior to GADCO's arrival, the land was "unused", thus also adopting the international "wasteland rhetoric" (see Alden Wily 2011). Whereas prior to the investment the legitimating discourses of women's empowerment were not relevant locally, now they were used by customary authorities to sell the investment to the local population and to women in particular. The corresponding legitimating narrative was adapted to the local setting, where the previous activities of women, in particular the collection of fuelwoods, were described as backbreaking, hard and primitive work. The fact that they could now pick the leftover rice from GADCO's fields was praised as a great economic opportunity for women (ignoring the fact that this was equally hard and backbreaking work).

2. **The high bargaining power of powerful local actors is a result of the favourable (inter)national institutional context. In other words, customary authorities in Ghana derive their power in the context of LSLA from (inter)national policy[1].**

In Ghana, current relations between chiefs and the state usually are analysed as power struggles in which the strength of chiefs often is attributed to a weakness of the state or the legal framework (Lavers and Boamah 2016). However, I argue that the power of today's customary authorities, especially in the current land rush, is still – just as it was during colonialism – a result of favourable (inter)national policies. The power of customary authorities thus needs to be analysed in conjunction with (inter)national policy rather than in opposition to state policy. Just as the British colonial power thought that it was necessary to have respected authorities with clearly defined land rights in order to allocate licenses to European mining and logging companies (Boni 2008, p. 90), today's (inter)national proponents of LSLAs – in the absence of private land owners – also need accepted authorities to negotiate and implement LSLAs. In the context of the (inter)national promotion of commercial agriculture through LSLAs, customary authorities, owing to their high bargaining power at the local level and to their strong position in customary land management, are in the best position to play this role.

The Ghanaian LAP is in line with the international policy shift from registering individual to registering customary land rights. Through the LAP, Customary Land Secretariats (CLSs) have been established with the intention of creating security of land tenure for smallholders while making it easier for investors to acquire land. As the case study has shown, this endeavour has led to a complete change in land tenure in the study area and to chiefs and clan heads taking control over land previously owned by families under customary law. In a context of increasing LSLAs, the codification of customary land rights and land titling through the LAP has created a massive power asymmetry between, on the one hand, those who through the project have been recognised as traditional landowners and have been given the authority to define and sanction local land rights and, on the other hand, those who depend on chiefs to get their rights acknowledged. Although the CLS fulfilled its role to help investors acquire land, land rights of individual land users and particularly members of settler communities were weakened.

In the Ghanaian context of institutional pluralism, both the Ghanaian state and foreign investors rely on strong chiefs in order to implement LSLAs and to translate the international investment logic – based on private property rights – into the complex customary setting which is characterised by multiple and at times overlapping and seasonally fluctuating rights over land and natural resources. Customary authorities are needed in order to "translate" international policies into the customary land tenure setting. However, because customary authorities are also deeply embedded in local power structures, LSLAs are bound to lead to a reinforcement of these mostly unequal power relations.

Chiefs (mis)use the CLS to map the boundaries of their own traditional areas while refusing to title individual parcels, intentionally keeping them open to interpretation (see also Ubink and Quan 2008). Through this strategy, they can defend their claims towards external actors (e.g. in the various court cases they are involved in) while keeping control over their subordinates. Through the CLS, the Ghanaian state (and the donors funding the LAP) back up and legitimise the actions of chiefs. This (inter)national reinforcement of customary authorities in the context of LSLAs leads to a shift in the perception of chiefs – from custodians of the land to landowners – and a consequent weakening of the rights of individual land users (see also Amanor 2008).

Although (inter)national policy regarding land and chieftaincy, including the LAP, is thus playing into the hands of chiefs and strengthening their position in the current land rush, I have also shown how district authorities are compelled to demonstrate that they have created an enabling investment environment. Thus, efforts to assert their authority in the investment process (i.e. through the imposition of a rice tax) have been largely unsuccessful. Furthermore, the general policy of non-interference in chieftaincy affairs and the close connections between some traditional authorities and the statutory ruling elite, as well as the fact that the districts are understaffed and underfunded, tie the hands of district authorities.

3. **The most successful customary authorities in the context of local institutional change are those who are best able to use the institutional context and related legitimating discourses and narratives to their advantage, performing "institution shopping".**

Chanock (1985), Mamdani (1996) and others have highlighted how different systems of traditional authority in Africa were much in flux prior to colonialism and that chieftaincy as it is known in many countries today was a colonial creation. As Chanock (1985, p. 237) points out: "Throughout the colonial period, as now, customary law was not the dead hand of tradition, but represented the responses of living interests". Oral history from the case study area confirms this. I have described how during colonialism power shifted away from different individual power holders (clan heads, war chiefs, stoolfathers etc.) to one clan, which took over all the newly created chieftaincy positions. Power struggles between different chiefs and subchiefs have been a key feature of the Fieve Traditional Area since colonial times and flared up again in the context of GADCO's acquisition.

Although the general strength of customary authorities in the current land rush can be seen as a result of the favourable policy environment, the question remains why certain traditional authorities have higher bargaining power than others and thus are more successful in promoting their own interests in the context of institutional transformation. By discussing the cases of a few powerful individuals, I aim to bring out the factors that provided them with increased bargaining power. First, I will look at the case of the Paramount Stoolfather, who was the main negotiation partner of GADCO. Then I will contrast the cases of two powerful women who were part of the committee in charge of disbursement of the community development fund with the case of the Paramount Queen Mother, who, even though she had a higher social status in the community, was left out of most decisions.

The Paramount Stoolfather – between tradition and modernity

The case study has highlighted how, as a result of the GADCO investment, colonially created conflicts between clans (i.e. the decision about which clan deserves to have the position of Paramount Chief) flared up again. Some decades ago, the clan of the Paramount Stoolfather – which during colonialism had taken up all newly created chieftaincy positions – had lost the position of Paramount Chief to another lineage. By claiming authority in the negotiations with GADCO, the Stoolfather now tried to gain prominence again. Although the Paramount Chief had originally negotiated the investment, the Stoolfather – by involving district authorities – managed to halt the implementation of the investment and to install himself as the main negotiation partner of the company. He also seemed to be a driving force behind the changes to the local land tenure system, which shifted control of land from families to the four clan heads (see Chapter 3).

During the many community meetings and during formal and informal interviews, it became clear that the Stoolfather not only had a very high level of education (PhD) and (as a lawyer) knew the (inter)national institutional context very well but also, through his status in the community, had in-depth knowledge of the community's history and traditions. He also had strong personal connections among not only the chieftaincy elite but also the national government elite. Although he often referred to oral history (i.e. to various events that established the importance of his clan and related customary institutions), he also evoked statutory institutions to legitimise his actions. In particular, he often mentioned the CLS, which – as he repeatedly emphasised – granted him and the other clan heads the "power of attorney" over all Fievie land. At community meetings, he skilfully combined references to the communities' ancestry and traditions with promises of development and modernity that the investment would bring. Within the favourable national policy context, he thus was able to successfully perform "institution shopping" to strengthen his own position in the process of local institutional change (see Haller 2010, 2013).

Women in the committee charged with disbursement of the community development fund – empowering women or powerful women?

As has been shown in the case study, although the customary setting in general and the GADCO negotiations in particular were dominated by men, two women stood out. One of them was a local Queen Mother from the lineage of the Paramount Stoolfather, and the other was a former assembly member. Although they both had a high social status – one due to her position in the customary setting and the other through her position in the statutory system – they both had a very good relationship with the Paramount Stoolfather. Furthermore, they were both highly educated and wealthy. It became clear that the educational background of both women, as well as their relevant connections to statutory and customary authorities, improved their ability to participate in "institution shopping". Whereas Yeboah and Bugri (2016) argue that the fact that women were part of the committee charged with disbursing GADCO's "community development fund" was important to get "women's voices" heard, my case study indicated that these women represented not "women" in general but a small elite.

It is also interesting to contrast the experience of the Paramount Queen Mother with those of the two women mentioned above. Although the customary status of the Paramount Queen Mother was higher than the status of the others, she was frequently left out of decisions and did not even know who was part of the committee in charge of disbursing the "community development fund". Unlike the other two women, she had no formal education and did not have a good understanding of statutory rules and regulations. She also did not have any relevant connections to the government elite.

What can be learned from these case descriptions?

The case descriptions above have shown that even though both (inter) national and local institutions provide certain people (i.e. chiefs, politicians and other wealthy men) with more power than others (i.e. women and members of settler communities), whether or not specific individuals can strategically use these institutions to further their own interests depends on their access to various other "bundles of power" (see Ribot and Peluso 2003), most importantly education (and specifically knowledge of different legal frameworks), social status and connections to influential people. The most successful person in the setting was the Paramount Stoolfather, who was highly educated and well connected and – most crucially – had in-depth knowledge of the (inter)national as well as the local institutional context. As a result, he was able to successfully perform "institution shopping" to strengthen his own position in the context of institutional change triggered by GADCO.

On the other hand, even though the local institutional context discriminated against women in many different ways, the fact that two women were part of the small group of beneficiaries from the GADCO investment again proves the importance of other "bundles of power" (in this case, wealth, education, social status and relevant connections), which helped these women overcome gender-based discrimination. The importance of adopting an intersectionality lens when analysing gender relations or women's discrimination is therefore essential, as women's positions differ according to class, age, lineage, education background, migration status and so on.

4. **Despite (inter)national win–win rhetoric, benefits and losses from the LSLA are distributed along intersectionally gendered power lines**[2].

(Inter)national agricultural and land policy generally envisage win–win situations arising from LSLAs, which are captured in various catchwords such as "sustainability", "poverty reduction" or "women's empowerment". However, policy actors and companies, rhetorically committed to gender equality, often reduce equality to a matter of numbers, seeking to include a certain percentage of women in their projects while disregarding local institutions and related resource rights as well as intersectionally gendered power relations. The case study has shown that inequality, including gender inequality, was pervasive in the Fievie Traditional Area and that, rather than challenging it, the GADCO investment simply empowered local elites and thus exacerbated power differentials. The various impacts of the GADCO investment aggravated existing inequalities in many ways:

a) *Settlers and women, who already had a lower status in customary societies, with regard to both land rights and decision-making, were most affected by the enclosure of farmland and common pool resources*: The farmland that the company enclosed was used mainly by settler communities, which were inadequately compensated if at all. Whereas some wealthier people were able to access new farmland through their families, many – women in particular – found their work reduced to exploitative sharecropping arrangements. In the future – as land scarcity increases – women likely will again be most vulnerable to land dispossession (see also Nyantaki-Frimpong and Bezner-Kerr 2017). Because much of the land leased by the company was previously used under a common property regime, people lost access to various common pool resources, in particular to fishponds, fuelwood and pastures, the latter two predominantly affecting settler communities and poorer women. Although the general policy discourse typically classifies these lands – the commons – as "wastelands" and LSLAs thus are praised for raising their productivity (see Alden Wily 2011), the present case study has shown that the privatisation of the commons happened at the expense of the most vulnerable members of society.

b) *Ecological and health consequences from unsustainable business practices were borne disproportionately by settler communities and women*: There is evidence that even though the company claimed to integrate "sustainability" into its business practices and has produced an Environmental Impact Statement and an Environmental Management Plan, it created several hazards for local communities, especially settler communities of Kpodzi and Kpevikpo. Adverse health and ecological effects were reported from the aerial spraying of pesticides and the destruction and poisoning of water ponds – and the consequences of these measures were borne disproportionately by women – those in charge of caring for the sick and fetching water from distant sources.

c) *Employment practices reinforced gendered stereotypes and discrimination*. Although GADCO's employment practices created a clear distinction between those working in the field and those working in offices (with major differences in pay), the local devaluation of women's work was also reinforced by the company. Women were found predominantly in the lowest-paid casual labour force. The gendered nature of employment created by GADCO reflects broader changes in the global economy, where employment is increasingly insecure and precarious and women usually are concentrated in the lowest ranks of the labour force (Kabeer 2012) – a fact that, however, is hailed as economic empowerment of women by neoliberal development actors and corporations (see Fraser 2009; Roberts 2015). Various authors have pointed out how casual agricultural labour is amongst the worst-paid jobs in many developing countries. It is usually chosen only as a strategy of last resort and predominantly by women (i.e. Oya 2010).

d) *Corporate social responsibility initiatives, such as the "community development fund" and the local outgrower scheme, got deeply entangled into local power structures, benefitting mostly the families of the chiefs.* Despite a great deal of positive press coverage for GADCO's community–private partnership, money from the community development fund was captured largely by the elite, including some powerful women. The company was able to congratulate itself for having recruited women into its outgrower scheme, although the outgrowers came mostly from the privileged chiefly families and favoured older farmers over the youth. Moreover, although many men were registered as outgrowers, it was mostly women who did the labour on the fields, thereby shouldering a considerable additional work and time burden. The claim to reduce poverty in the area, in particular through the outgrower scheme, can easily be refuted. Most outgrowers hailed from wealthy families, and many even subcontracted poor villagers to work on the fields for them. Furthermore, it was striking that in an area of high youth unemployment, hardly any young people were involved in the scheme.

In line with Intersectionality Studies (Cho et al. 2013; Cooper 2016), I have tried to avoid the trap of homogenising local women and men. Although the local institutional context clearly discriminated against women in many ways (i.e. with regard to land rights, decision-making and employment) and dominant notions of masculinities and femininities further decreased women's choices and increased their time burden (i.e. through their responsibilities for domestic and care work), the way that individual women were affected by this context depended on various other factors (i.e. wealth, social status, education and close connections to the customary elite). The institutional structures in place certainly contributed to make women more vulnerable in the face of LSLAs (see also Levien 2017), but it is simplistic to assume that all women lose out. The case study has shown that some women were able to overcome discriminatory institutional barriers and benefit considerably from the investment. However, it became clear that although their gender rhetoric may have helped GADCO to access international funding, the simplified slogans used by policy makers and investors alike – whereby market integration equates to "women's empowerment" – are faulty, as they lack an appraisal of the social and institutional context and the different intersecting power relations in which women and men are embedded. Most of the women who benefitted from the GADCO investment were already "empowered" prior to the investment.

5. **Adaptation and resistance to the LSLA are also shaped by the institutional setting and the relative bargaining power of individuals, and gender plays an important role.**

Chapter 5 showed that it was mainly men who engaged in different types of resistance – from small individual acts (i.e. stealing, destroying the company's machines, and pulling out demarcations) to violence (men from Bakpa Adzani arming themselves), to the writing of petitions to chiefs and government officials (cattle herders) or to submitting the case to the court (men from Bakpa Adzani and fishpond owners). This can be explained by the local institutional setting, as men had "ownership" of resources (women had only use rights), as well as by prevalent notions of masculinity, which allowed men to speak up and use physical force (both of which were unacceptable for women).

The institutional setting also determined the type of resistance chosen by Bakpa settlers. Because they, being settlers, had no voice in the local customary setting and their land rights were not even recognised by state authorities, their only option was violence. The type of resistance that men engaged in also related to their bargaining power. Poorer and less influential members of society were more likely to use "weapons of the weak" (Scott 1985), like stealing or pulling out demarcations, whereas influential and educated members of society were more likely to write petitions, engage in court cases or involve the media.

Because women traditionally were required to feed their families, the pressure of adapting to the changed circumstances was felt strongly by them. It has been shown that many women thus started to collect the leftover rice from the company's fields – initially also an act of defiance and resistance, as it was forbidden to enter the fields. After a while, the illegal picking was allowed by the company and chiefs. Although this could be seen as a successful act of resistance, it is questionable whether being allowed to pick up the company's waste can really be called a success. It is also telling that in an investment claiming to empower women, women are reduced to tediously picking up the leftovers of the product supposed to bring development and wealth for all.

Adaptation strategies also differed according to wealth, social status and relevant connections. Whereas individuals from wealthy, landowning families could easily access new farmland, many – especially poorer women – had to fall back on sharecropping arrangements.

Similarly, those with close connections to the customary elite were more likely to be considered for outgrower positions or employment, thus helping them to adapt to the changed circumstances.

6. **The shift from common to de facto private property and the enclosure of many common pool resources reduce the adaptation capacities, especially of the weakest members of society.**

Livelihoods in the study area have been transformed several times in the past. It has been shown that prior to the construction of the Akosombo Dam in the 1960s, several of the study communities used to depend on the Volta River and its seasonal flooding cycles, and rights to different resources varied according to the season. Everyday life was strongly disrupted by the building of the dam, and to cope with the changed situation, aggrieved parties adopted different strategies, ranging from increased reliance on farming and trading to migration. However, in a context which was also increasingly unpredictable because of climatic changes, the floodplains and adjoining pasture areas continued to offer important resources to local people's livelihoods, including fish, pasture and fuelwood. In particular, female-headed households and poorer community members relied on these open-access areas, as the sale of firewood and charcoal constituted a major income-earning opportunity for them.

Prior to GADCO's arrival, large tracts of land thus were managed under a common property regime and land that could be used for the expansion of farming activities was already concentrated in the hands of a few families. The GADCO investment therefore has to be seen in a context where livelihoods were increasingly difficult because of climatic changes and increased scarcity of land. The investment added stress to an already-difficult livelihood situation. As shown in Chapter 5, most villagers were able to adapt once more to the changed circumstances, but adaptation strategies also led to increased land scarcity and conflicts. Furthermore, many people became partly or wholly dependent on the company to sustain their livelihoods, be it through employment, outgrowing or the gleaning of rice from the company's fields. Although in some cases their income from these activities was greater than the income generated from the land and resources they were using before, the legitimate fear that the company could leave at any moment made them vulnerable. This was also evident in the time between GADCO's bankruptcy and the takeover by RMG Concept, when many women complained that there was no more rice available and they could not go back to cutting the trees for fuelwood as most trees were gone.

Notably, the loss of common pool resources and the complete dependency on the company are bound to reduce the villagers' resilience in the face of possible future shocks (i.e. another bankruptcy). Similarly, the company's agricultural practices, which revolved around mono-cropping and heavy use of fertilizers with no fallow periods, are likely to significantly reduce soil fertility and may make the land unsuitable for small-scale farming activities in the uncertain future. So it is feasible to think of the company's operations in terms not only of "land grabbing" but also of "resilience-grabbing", as has been suggested by Haller et al. (2020).

Policy lessons

Although GADCO has been hailed as a "best practice" example of an LSLA, the case study has confirmed many of LSLAs' negative outcomes found in a broad range of other studies. This allows me to extrapolate my research outcomes and make proposals for business-led developments more broadly. It shows that LSLAs are unlikely to generate sustainable social or environmental improvements and above all to create gender equality if investors do not keep in view existing power relations and institutional mechanisms, which regulate access to resources. Acting responsibly as an investor and development actor cannot be reduced to setting numeric goals of inclusion. Companies need to engage with the concerned communities, aware of intersectional power structures. This means that setting gender quotas is not enough. Meaningful engagement with diverse local stakeholders – ideally mediated by a "neutral" external person (i.e. non-governmental organisation [NGO] collaborator and academics) – is necessary for business-led initiatives to become more responsible.[3]

Governmental agencies, private charitable foundations, development banks or philanthropists who support business initiatives such as GADCO have a responsibility. They should not rely on short field trips, papers and the embellished internet presence of a company in order to evaluate a project and decide about financial support. Smiling, happy women in lush green fields do not reflect the reality on site. Long-term, in-depth engagement with the companies and especially the communities is needed in order to hold businesses accountable and push for meaningful changes. Connecting the donors more closely not only to the companies they support but also to the involved communities or local NGOs would create a system of checks and balances from which all parties could benefit in the end.

Further research

Much research on LSLAs has been conducted at the micro level, and a large number of case studies have outlined the disruptive consequences of LSLAs on local livelihoods. Although my own case study confirms many of the negative effects that have been described by others, I have tried to connect the local level to the national and the international levels by emphasising the importance of (inter)national policies and legitimating ideologies in the current land rush. I believe that, in the future, more research should be conducted at the level of international and national governance. One must understand how prominent "public–private partnership" agreements, such as the New Alliance for Food Security and Nutrition, operate in order to lay open the motivations and interests of the different stakeholders in these alliances and to expose which networks they rely on to disseminate powerful legitimating discourses and narratives and thus to influence public opinion.

Furthermore, the operations, motivations and funding structures of specific companies should be analysed in more detail. Simultaneously, there needs to be more research on resistance to LSLAs at the local level and on resistance of social movements aiming to change (inter)national institutions and ideologies. How do these movements interact with different policy and corporate actors? How are their demands met, integrated or misused in political and corporate strategies? Long-term multi-site ethnographic field research with these different (inter)national actors seems to be particularly well suited to get a detailed understanding of how specific institutions and legitimating discourses and narratives, which make LSLAs possible, are fabricated and hopefully also changed.

Notes

1 This subchapter is based on the article by Lanz, K., Gerber, J.D. and T. Haller (2018). 'Land Grabbing, the State and Chiefs: The politics of extending commercial agriculture in Ghana'. *Development and Change* 49 (6): 1526–52.
2 This subchapter is based on the article by Lanz, K., Prügl, E. and J.D. Gerber (2020). 'The poverty of neoliberalized feminism: Gender equality in a "best practice" large-scale land investment in Ghana'. *Journal of Peasant Studies* 47 (3): 525–43.
3 The constitutionality approach developed by Haller et al. (2016) outlines some important characteristics that could be useful in such a process, namely participatory processes of negotiation, acknowledgement of pre-existing institutions as a basis for institution building, outside catalyzing agents, recognition of local knowledge, and higher-level acknowledgment of the newly created institutions.

References

Alden Wily, L. (2011). 'The law is to blame. The vulnerable status of common property rights in sub-Saharan Africa'. *Development and Change* 42 (3): 357–79.

Amanor, K.S. (2008). 'The changing face of customary land tenure'. In Ubink, J.M. and K.S. Amanor (eds.), *Contesting land and custom in Ghana: State, chief and citizen*. Leiden, The Netherlands: Leiden University Press, pp. 55–81.

Boni, S. (2008). 'Traditional ambiguities and authoritarian interpretations in Sefwi land disputes'. In Ubink, J.M. and K.S. Amanor (eds.), *Contesting land and custom in Ghana: State, chief and citizen*. Leiden, The Netherlands: Leiden University Press, pp. 81–112.

Chanock, M. (1985). *Law, custom and social order: The colonial experience in Malawi and Zambia*. Cambridge, UK: Cambridge University Press.

Cho, S., Crenshaw, K.W. and L. McCall. (2013). 'Toward a field of intersectionality studies: Theory, applications, and praxis'. *Signs: Journal of Women in Culture and Society* 38 (4): 785–810.

Cooper, B. (2016). 'Intersectionality'. In Disch, L. and M. Mawkesworth (eds.), *The Oxford handbook of feminist theory*. Oxford, UK: Oxford University Press.

Ferguson, J. (1994). *The anti-politics machine: "Development", depoliticization and bureaucratic power in Lesotho*. Minneapolis: University of Minnesota Press.

Ferguson, J. (2006). *Global Shadows. Africa in the neoliberal world order*. London: Duke University Press.

Fraser, N. (2009). 'Feminism, capitalism and the cunning of history'. *New Left Review* 56: 97–117.

Haller, T., ed. (2010). *Disputing the floodplains: Institutional change and the politics of resource management in African floodplains*. Leiden, The Netherlands: Brill.

Haller, T. (2013). *The contested floodplain: Institutional change of the commons in the Kafue Flats, Zambia*. Lanham, MD: Rowman & Littlefield.

Haller, T., Acciaioli, G. and S. Rist (2016). 'Constitutionality: Conditions for crafting local ownership of institution-building processes'. *Society & Natural Resources* 29 (1): 68–87.

Haller, T., Ngutu, M. and F. Käser (2020). 'Does commons grabbing lead to resilience grabbing? The anti-politics machine of neo-liberal agrarian development and local responses'. *Land*, Special issue. doi:10.3390/books978-3-03943-840-2

Hoogvelt, A. (1997). *Globalization and the post-colonial world: The new political economy of development*. London: Macmillan.

Kabeer, N. (2012). *Women's economic empowerment and inclusive growth: Labour markets and enterprise development*. Ottawa, ON: International Development Research Institute (IDRC).

Lanz, K., Gerber, J.D. and T. Haller (2018). 'Land grabbing, the state and chiefs: The politics of extending commercial agriculture in Ghana'. *Development and Change* 49 (6): 1526–52.

Lanz, K., Prügl, E. and J.D. Gerber (2020). 'The poverty of neoliberalized feminism: Gender equality in a "best practice" large-scale land investment in Ghana'. *Journal of Peasant Studies* 47 (3): 525–43.

Lavers, T. and F. Boamah (2016). 'The impact of agricultural investments on state capacity: A comparative analysis of Ethiopia and Ghana'. *Geoforum* 72: 94–103.

Levien, M. (2017). 'Gender and land dispossession'. *Journal of Peasant Studies* 44 (6): 1111–34.

Mamdani, M. (1996). *Citizen and subject: Contemporary Africa and the legacy of late colonialism.* Princeton, NJ: Princeton University Press.

Nyantaki-Frimpong, H. and R. Bezner-Kerr (2017). 'Land grabbing, social differentiation, intensified migration and food security in Northern Ghana'. *Journal of Peasant Studies* 44 (2): 421–44.

Oya, C. (2010). *Rural inequality, wage employment and labour market formation in Africa: Historical and micro-level evidence.* Working Paper 97. Geneva, Switzerland: ILO.

Ribot, J.C. and N.L. Peluso (2003). 'A theory of access'. *Rural Sociology* 68 (2): 153–81.

Roberts, A. (2015). 'The political economy of "transnational business feminism": Problematizing the corporate-led gender equality agenda'. *International Feminist Journal of Politics* 17 (2): 209–31.

Scott, J.C. (1985). *Weapons of the weak: Everyday forms of peasant resistance.* New Haven, CT: Yale University Press.

Ubink, J.M. and J.F. Quan (2008). 'How to combine tradition and modernity? Regulating customary land management in Ghana'. *Land Use Policy* 25 (2): 198–213.

Yeboah, E. and J. Bugri (2016). 'Building innovative partnership to bridge gender gaps in large scale land investments, insights from the GADCO – Fievie model in Ghana'. Paper presented at the *Annual World Bank Conference on Land and Poverty*, Washington, DC (14–18 March 2016).

7 Epilogue

From research to action

Considering myself to be a critical feminist anthropologist, I found it key to continually reflect on my own positionality and values and to engage with my research participants beyond the formal research process (see also Ackerly and True 2010; Haraway 1988). A researcher's identity (in terms of nationality, age, gender, sexuality etc.) clearly plays a key role in the research process and his/her* interactions, which often are marked by huge power differentials (Beer 2003, p. 55). This certainly was the case with me – a young, white and privileged woman conducting research in a rather patriarchal, conservative and underprivileged society. Not only was I myself constantly aware of the power, wealth and knowledge gap between me and the vast majority of locals I came in touch with on a daily basis, but people also ascribed to me a certain identity (wealthy, rich and emancipated) which was difficult to contest. So an important part of keeping a research diary was also to reflect on my own positionality and the way it affected my interactions with people.

As is customary in Ghanaian society, I first had to get permission from the chiefs to conduct research in their villages. Initially, all chiefs were very friendly and helpful and I started my research by conducting several expert interviews with some of the main chiefs and government officials. Although this helped to establish the trust of the elite, it created a great deal of suspicion within the local community. As I later learned, many locals thought that I was part of either the Global Agri-Development Company (GADCO) or another investment company trying to acquire land. Even as I was seen more often in the villages and started to conduct group discussions and individual interviews, this suspicion did not immediately vanish. Countless times, I had to explain what I was doing and where I was from before people started slowly opening up to me. I noticed that trust had finally been established when villagers started to openly discuss their relations with customary authorities with

DOI: 10.4324/9781003212768-7

me. As chiefs are supposed to be in direct contact with ancestors and thus should not be criticised, most interview respondents initially were very guarded when it came to discussing chieftaincy matters with me. A strong dissatisfaction with (some) chiefs became apparent and was openly discussed only after trust had been established.

Researching a contested topic

As Cramer et al. (2015) highlight in their account of field research on large-scale land acquisitions (LSLAs) in Ethiopia and Uganda, considerable dangers and difficulties are involved in conducting research on a politically contested topic. Although the different incidences during fieldwork recounted by these authors include imprisonment of the researchers and even attempted murder by villagers who did not understand the motives of the researchers, my own experiences were not as extreme but nevertheless included moments where I feared for the safety of myself and my family. At times, it was also hard to judge the situation, especially during the first field research, as the company was trying to expand its operations and several death threats were issued against company representatives and physical fights between villagers and company representatives broke out on the company's ground.

Although getting the consent of local chiefs and district officials at the beginning of the research initially bought me their trust, this happened at the expense of the trust from the community. As my research continued and local people were opening up more and more to me and I was also getting more engaged, the tables were turned. Several incidents revealed that I had become a suspect to chiefs as well as to the company. On several occasions, I was asked by local chiefs and by company representatives to show them my questionnaires and to hand in all video material to them. I was also repeatedly told that I should be aware that the people I was interviewing were lying to me about the difficulties caused by the LSLA since they were expecting handouts from me. Similarly, a company representative told me that I was interviewing the wrong people and that my methodology was not sound since I had not interviewed him (even though I had interviewed several company representatives and the general manager on diverse occasions). During the second field research, I was told by some outgrowers and employees that everybody had been briefed by the new company management not to provide me with any information.

Although initially some chiefs as well as the company's general manager appeared to be surprisingly honest, as the research proceeded they were clearly trying to influence my findings by foregrounding only positive aspects of the LSLA and at times obviously not telling the truth and contradicting what they had said on earlier occasions. At the same time, it became clear that some of the local interview respondents, in particular in Bakpa Adzani, were trying to influence my findings by exaggerating their difficulties. Cramer et al. (2015) recount similar research experiences on LSLA, emphasising how locally dominant individuals and organisations tried to restrict their access to the field and influence their findings. They highlight how

> fieldwork then becomes embroiled in the political economy it is trying to understand. When research becomes part of the tussle of interests, ideas, and institutions, clearly this may constrain research and shape findings, but it may also reveal that local political economy in sharper contrast.
>
> (p. 147)

This was certainly the case in my research, as the contested nature of the LSLA became obvious and power lines in the community, as well as the positions of different groups and individuals, became apparent. However, the longer I stayed in the area, the more entangled I became in the local conflict and the more compelled I felt to take a position in it, as will be shown below.

Becoming entangled – from research to advocacy

As described above, researching a highly controversial and conflict-laden phenomenon such as LSLA, I added another layer to the politicised context, as different groups were trying to "use" my presence to emphasise and amplify their own position. Although I initially stayed out of the conflict over the expansion of GADCO, it became more and more difficult not to take sides and to watch injustices unfold. As I was listening to more and more people's stories and was asked again and again what I could do to help them, the idea of holding a large research dissemination meeting, where some of the preliminary results were shared and discussed, came to my mind. As an outsider who nonetheless had spent a considerable amount of time in the local area and had spoken to a large number of different people, I was seen by most of the locals as a "neutral" and trustworthy person who could pass on the grievances articulated by various respondents to the company, chiefs and government representatives with a certain amount of authority. By organising these meetings, I moved away from purely academic anthropology to advocacy anthropology – or, in the words of Kellet (2009, p. 23), "from detachment to engagement". According to Kirsch (2002, p. 178), advocacy is a "logical extension of the commitment to reciprocity that underlies the practice of anthropology".

With the help of my research assistant, a large dissemination meeting, which included various speakers from both government and traditional authorities and was framed by a programme of music, prayers and food, was organised in Fievie-Dugame. In the main part of the meeting, my research assistant gave a speech about women's statutory land rights in Ghana and I gave a speech outlining preliminary research results and providing concrete recommendations to improve the situation. The meeting was attended by over 200 persons, including many chiefs, government officials and one company representative. Numerous people who had participated in the research, as well as other interested villagers from Fievie-Dugame, Kpodzi and Kpevikpo, showed up[1].

Although the intervention on women's land rights led to interesting discussions among participants, my own speech solicited only a few comments by a company representative, a chief and an elderly "honorary citizen". So it was very difficult to judge what the majority of listeners thought of the speech. When a few people approached me after the meeting and said they were very happy that I had come to the area and held this speech, it became clear that – even though my idea was to host a "democratic meeting" where everybody could discuss my results – local power relations did not just disappear and most participants were scared to speak up in public.

The general perception of the meeting became evident only when I came back for the second research period two years later. This time, I was very warmly welcomed by all communities and many villagers approached me, telling me that they really liked what I was doing and that they were happy to give me any information I needed. I did not intend to hold a second dissemination meeting, but about two weeks before my departure, a group of young women and men complained bitterly about their deteriorating living conditions and asked whether I could organise another meeting, which they wanted to use as a platform to address their chiefs and criticise them for not keeping the promises they had made at the first meeting. After I consulted with my research assistant, we decided to go ahead and thus organised a meeting within a very short time. Owing to the short notice, fewer people attended. However, out of the roughly 30 participants, three were chiefs and eight were government officials.

As at the first meeting, both my research assistant and I gave a speech. My research assistant started by giving his input on the Ghana

Commercial Agriculture Project (GCAP) Community/Investor Guidelines for Large-scale Land Acquisitions and then I gave my own input on the preliminary results of the second research period. After the meeting, many people came to thank me and asked for a copy of my speech. I was furthermore asked by a moderator of the local radio station South Tongu Radio to participate in a radio programme the next day. Because I was already leaving the area on the same day, my research assistant attended on my behalf. According to several conversations with my research assistant, after the dissemination meeting, young men in Fievie came together to confront the chiefs directly. The young men not only demanded to know what the money from the "community development fund" had been used for but also wanted to be represented in all aspects of GADCO's operations (i.e. employment, the outgrower scheme and the rice mill). As a result, one person was employed at the mill, but no other changes took place.

Back home – the engagement continues

I continued to stay in touch with my research assistant long after having handed in my doctoral dissertation, and he provided me with frequent updates of the situation in the various villages. For some time, I played with the idea of contacting the Swiss owners of GADCO to confront them with my research results. When I started working for Alliance Sud, a political umbrella organisation of Swiss non-governmental organisations, trying to influence Swiss policy towards global justice, the opportunity finally arose. In 2019, I partnered up with one of our funding organisations – Bread for All – which has helped several communities in Africa claim their rights in the face of land grabs. Before contacting the CEO of RMG Concept (the company that had taken over GADCO), I discussed with my research assistant what concrete demands we could make. Given the fact that many of the problems caused by the investment could not be resolved in the short to medium term, we decided to ask the CEO to construct a bridge over the canal that the company had built outside Kpevikpo, as without it the village often remained isolated from neighbouring communities and whenever there was water in the canal, children could not go to school, women could not get to the market, and people were cut off from social services or unable to attend meetings.

During a phone call, the CEO agreed to attend a meeting with the affected villagers. On the appointed day, he was supposed to fetch my research assistant, who had organised the meeting, in order for them to drive together to Kpevikpo. However, instead of driving straight to the village, he took my assistant to the nearby GADCO office, where several representatives of the traditional authorities were waiting. They berated him as a manipulator and vilified him for his role in the research, threatening him with legal action. (Later, I also received a letter from the traditional authorities discrediting my research and threatening both of us with legal action.)

After this unpleasant encounter in the GADCO office, the group nonetheless proceeded to the community meeting, taking the chiefs along. There, after listening to the local people, the GADCO CEO finally agreed to the erection of a bridge and promised to provide every household in Kpevikpo with solar panels. After many emails and some back-and-forth, the bridge was finally built in July 2020. However, the people are still awaiting the promised solar panels.

Although I temporarily feared for the safety of my research assistant, he remains very adamant that we have done nothing wrong and continues to advocate for the rights of the affected communities. I, for my part, am happy that I could contribute to an improvement, however modest, through my research and advocacy work.

Note

1 Owing to the conflict between the Fievie Traditional Area and the two Bakpa communities, I could not invite people from Bakpa Adzani to these meetings. However, they were informed of the meetings.

References

Ackerly, B. and J. True (2010). 'Back to the future: Feminist theory, activism, and doing feminist research in the age of globalization'. *Women's Studies International Forum* 33: 464–72.

Beer, B., ed. (2003). *Methoden ethnologischer Feldforschung*. Berlin: Dietrich Reimer Verlag.

Cramer, C., Johnston, D., Oya, C. and J. Sender (2015). 'Research note. Mistakes, crises, and research independence: The perils of fieldwork as a form of evidence'. *African Affairs* 115 (458): 145–60.

Haraway, D. (1988). 'Situated knowledges: The science question in feminism and the privilege of partial perspective'. *Feminist Studies* 14 (3): 575–99.

Kellet, P. (2009). 'Advocacy in anthropology: Active engagement or passive scholarship?' *Durham Anthropology Journal* 16 (1): 22–31.

Kirsch, S. (2002). 'Anthropology and advocacy: A case study of the campaign against the Ok Tedi mine'. *Critique of Anthropology* 22: 175–200.

Milton Keynes UK
Ingram Content Group UK Ltd.
UKHW022041190124
436364UK00007B/73